# INTERACTIVE CITATION WORKBOOK FOR *THE BLUEBOOK: A UNIFORM SYSTEM OF CITATION*

## 2008 Edition

# LEXISNEXIS MATTHEW BENDER LAW SCHOOL ADVISORY BOARD

# INTERACTIVE CITATION WORKBOOK FOR *THE BLUEBOOK: A UNIFORM SYSTEM OF CITATION*

## 2008 Edition

---

Tracy L. McGaugh
*Associate Professor of Legal Process*
*Touro Law Center*

Christine Hurt
*Professor of Law*
*University of Illinois College of Law*

LexisNexis®

ISBN: 978–1–4224–2393–6


Editorial Offices
744 Broad Street, Newark, NJ 07102 (973) 820-2000
201 Mission St., San Francisco, CA 94105-1831 (415) 908-3200
www.lexisnexis.com

MATTHEW BENDER

(2008–Pub.3125)

# TABLE OF CONTENTS

# *TABLE OF CONTENTS*

# *ACKNOWLEDGMENTS*

It takes a village to create the ICW! The ICW is made possible by the tremendous support we receive from our families, friends, research assistants, secretaries and law schools. Specifically we would like to thank University of Illinois College of Law and Touro Law Center, and of course, our first-year law students. We are especially indebted to Sean Caldwell at LexisNexis for ushering us into the next phase of the ICW.

# *USING THE INTERACTIVE CITATION WORKBOOK*

## Layout of the Workbook

The ICW contains eighteen citation exercises. Each exercise builds on and reinforces the skills learned in previous exercises. The goal of this learning method is for you to become familiar with the organization and use of *The Bluebook: A Uniform System of Citation* (currently in its Eighteenth Edition).*

You need not memorize the citation rules. However, through repeated use, you will probably find that you have memorized the commonly-used rules.

Each ICW chapter consists of explanatory text and a citation exercise. The text will introduce and explain the rules needed for that exercise, demonstrate by example how those rules are used, and give a checklist you can use in drafting your citations for that exercise. Because each exercise builds on previous exercises, you might find each checklist helpful for many of the later exercises as well. The exercises may be completed in the Workbook and turned in, or you may transfer your answers to the Workstation for immediate feedback. Check with your instructor to see which method you should use.

## Beginning to Use *The Bluebook*

*The Bluebook* is divided into several major sections. To help you navigate it more easily, you may want to tab the sections of *The Bluebook* you will use most: Bluepages, Cases, Statutes, Table 1, Table 6, and the Index. Before you begin any ICW exercises, you should read the Introduction to *The Bluebook*. Pay particular attention to the section titled "Structure of *The Bluebook*." Although the index gets only a one-sentence mention at the end of that section, the index can be tremendously helpful to you. If you have a question about drafting a citation, and you have no idea where to start, the index is your best bet. The Eighteenth Edition index is color-coded so that references that appear in text are in black; those that appear in examples are in blue.

## Getting Started on the Exercises

The Interactive Citation Workbook and Workstation (both "ICW") will help you learn the citation rules you will use most frequently when you clerk for a law firm or a court and, later, practice law. The ICW does not cover the rules that most practitioners rarely, if ever, use. However, after completing the ICW exercises, you should be comfortable enough with *The Bluebook* as a reference guide that you can find rules you need to cite any authority.

Because the ICW focuses on citation rules used by practitioners of the law, you will use the typeface conventions that practitioners use. These are found in the Bluepages. You will notice that the examples in the main body of *The Bluebook* rarely follow the typeface instructions in the Bluepages. The reason is that *The Bluebook* examples use the

---

* Excerpts from *The Bluebook* used with permission of the copyright holders: Columbia Law Review, The Harvard Law Review Association, University of Pennsylvania Law Review, and the Yale Law Journal.

typeface conventions for law review citations (Rule 2.1) rather than court documents and legal memoranda. Take a moment now to read B13 on Typeface Conventions on pages 23 and 24 of the Bluebook.

Here are a few things you will need to know for every citation exercise:

- The Bluepages tip at the top of page 4 allows for either underlining or *italicizing* certain parts of a citation. The Workstation, however, will allow you only to italicize. You cannot useLARGE AND SMALL CAPS in the ICW because the typeface conventions in the Bluepages do not allow for large and small caps.
- Rule 6.1(a) tells you when to leave a space between abbreviations and when not to.
- Rule 2.1(f) tells you when punctuation should be italicized.

Students are often eager to "jump in" and complete the online exercises, skipping either the workbook text or *The Bluebook* rules. However, because many of the examples in the workbook and *The Bluebook* are similar to the online problems, students often find that reviewing examples is faster than going it alone.

**Using the Interactive Citation Workstation**

You may complete your exercises online. Your professor should tell you whether this is a requirement or not. The Interactive Citation Workstation (ICW) will give you immediate feedback on the citations you draft for these exercises. Probably, the bulk of the time you spend on the ICW exercises will be in drafting your first attempt at the citation. Therefore, if you share a computer with someone or are billed for Internet access on the basis of the amount of time spent online, you may want to do the initial work on paper to minimize your time online.

When you finish the results online, you can e-mail those results to your professor from the ICW, or you can print out the results. If you e-mail the results, it is still a good idea to print and keep a copy of the results as confirmation that you completed an exercise and to use as a personal reference or study guide.

The ICW is located at http://lexisnexis.com/icw/. The complete instructions for using the Workstation are on the web site. To save time in completing the exercises, you should read these online instructions before beginning the first exercise online.

# Chapter 1
# CASE NAMES

Legal citation, like citation in other disciplines, identifies the source of an idea that a writer uses in his or her writing. A legal citation to a judicial opinion (a "case") has three basic components, all of which are given in the heading of every judicial opinion: the case name, the volume and page number of the source the opinion is printed in (the "reporter"), and a parenthetical that includes the identification of the court that issued the opinion and the date of the opinion. The first three exercises of the ICW will acquaint you with how to use the information given in the heading of an opinion to draft a basic legal citation. As you read the text in each ICW chapter, you may find it helpful to refer to *The Bluebook* rules mentioned so you can familiarize yourself with both the content and location of the rules. This 2007 edition of the ICW follows the most recent edition of *The Bluebook*, the eighteenth edition. Also, the examples provided in *The Bluebook* following each rule will be helpful in understanding the rule itself.

The "formula" for a basic legal citation follows:

***Party 1 v. Party 2***, Vol. Reporter Pg. (Court Date).

*The Bluebook* quick reference for a case name in a citation is B5.1.1 of the Bluepages.

## A. Using Typeface

The first part of a citation is the case name (*Party 1 v. Party 2*). The case name is made up of the names of the parties. Looking at the citation formula above, you will notice that the case name (*Party 1 v. Party 2*) is italicized. This follows B5.1.1 and B13 of the Bluepages, which allows for either *italicizing* or <u>underlining</u> the entire case name. When you type your citations in the ICW, you will use italics. Otherwise, you should check with your instructor or supervising attorney for his or her preference. What you might not notice at first glance is that the comma following the case name is *not* italicized. This follows the B5.1.1 Bluepages tip, which tells you not to italicize punctuation when it *follows* italicized material. Italicize punctuation only if it is *within* the italicized material.

## B. Shortening Party Information

The party information is given at the beginning of a court opinion in the heading. You should list parties in the order they are given in the heading, regardless of procedural posture (*e.g.*, if the defendant is listed first in the heading, list him or her first in the citation). Because cases may involve multiple parties, one or more of which may have a lengthy name, *The Bluebook* provides a system of rules for shortening the case name so that the citation to an opinion is not cumbersome yet still sufficiently identifies the primary parties. These rules are found in 10.2.1 and 10.2.2 with some additional guidance on abbreviations coming from Table 6 (T.6) and Table 10 (T.10) in the blue pages at the back of *The Bluebook*.

Rules 10.2.1 and 10.2.2 fall into two general categories: rules calling for omissions and rules calling for abbreviations. The rules for abbreviation differ slightly for citation sentences than those for textual sentences. A citation sentence is a citation that follows a proposition and stands on its own.

False imprisonment is the willful detention of another without that person's consent and without the authority of law. ***Employer v. Employee*, 123 Rptr. 456 (Ct. 2000).**

A textual sentence is the proposition itself and may include a citation within it.

In ***Employer v. Employee*, 123 Rptr. 456 (Ct. 2000)**, the court held that false imprisonment is the willful detention of another without that person's consent and without the authority of law.

The citation rules of omission apply to case names in both citation and textual sentences. However, the citation rules of abbreviation apply primarily to case names in citation sentences. In a textual sentence, the case name is abbreviated according to only Rule 10.2.1(c) without regard to the abbreviations listed in T.6 and T.10.

Read the rules of omission and abbreviation in 10.2.1 and 10.2.2 carefully before attempting the Case Names exercise. Study the examples to help you understand the rules.

You **should omit** the following general types of information from the citation:

- any actions other than the first in a consolidated case (10.2.1(a))
- any parties other than the first listed on each side (10.2.1(a))
- phrases indicating multiple parties (10.2.1(a))
- procedural phrases (10.2.1(b))
- the word "The" when it is the first word of a party name (10.2.1(d))
- descriptive terms that describe a party already identified by name (10.2.1(e))
- "State of," "Commonwealth of," and "People of," unless the party name is the same as the state the opinion is from. In that case, use only "State," "Commonwealth," or "People" (10.2.1(f)) [1]
- "City of" unless it begins a party name (10.2.1(f))
- prepositional phrases of location not following "City," or like expressions (10.2.1(f))
- "of America" after "United States" (10.2.1(f))
- given names or initials of *individuals* unless they are part of a business name (10.2.1(g))
- "Inc.," "Ltd.," "L.L.C.," "N.A.," "F.S.B.," and similar terms if other words in the name *clearly* indicate that the party is a business (10.2.1(h))
- "of Internal Revenue" from "Commissioner of Internal Revenue" (10.2.1(j))

You **should abbreviate** words in a citation in the following circumstances:

- "versus" is abbreviated to "v."
- when the word is listed in 10.2.1(c) or T.6 (10.2.1(c) and 10.2.2)
- when the word is a state, country, or other geographical unit listed in T.10 unless the unit is a named party (10.2.2)
- when the word is listed in 10.2.1(c) if your citation is in *either* a citation or textual sentence

You **may abbreviate** words in a citation sentence in the following circumstances:

[1] When the government entity is referred to as "The People of the State of" or "The Commonwealth of the People of the," the appropriate abbreviations are "People" and "Commonwealth" respectively.

- when the word is eight letters or more if (i) the abbreviation would save substantial space, and (ii) the abbreviation would clearly refer to the party named (10.2.2)
- when the full name of a party can be abbreviated to widely recognized initials (10.2.1(c)). In that case, you would not include periods in the abbreviation according to 6.1(b)

You **should not abbreviate** the following:

- states, countries, and other geographical units listed in T.10 and named as parties (10.2.2)
- "United States" (10.2.2)
- any word not listed in 10.2.1(c) *if the citation is in a **textual** sentence*

When drafting a case name, first omit the necessary information and then abbreviate the rest. Let's try an example of a case name in a citation sentence and then in a textual sentence before you tackle the Case Names exercise.

Southwest Engineering Company and John Doe, Defendants-Appellants, versus The United States of America, Plaintiff-Appellee

First, let's **omit** all information that the rules require. Rule 10.2.1(a) requires that we omit all parties other than the first, so we will omit "and John Doe" from the first party:

Southwest Engineering Company ~~and John Doe~~, Defendants-Appellants, versus The United States of America, Plaintiff-Appellee

Rule 10.2.1(e) requires that we omit descriptive terms for named parties, so we will delete "Defendants-Appellants" and "Plaintiff-Appellee":

Southwest Engineering Company ~~and John Doe, Defendants-Appellants,~~ versus The United States of America~~, Plaintiff-Appellee~~

Rule 10.2.1(d) requires that we omit "The" when it is the first word of a party name, so we will omit it from "The United States of America":

Southwest Engineering Company ~~and John Doe, Defendants-Appellants,~~ versus ~~The~~ United States of America~~, Plaintiff-Appellee~~

Rule 10.2.1(f) requires that we omit "of America" after "United States":

Southwest Engineering Company ~~and John Doe, Defendants-Appellants,~~ versus ~~The~~ United States ~~of America, Plaintiff-Appellee~~

Now that we have omitted all of the words *The Bluebook* requires, let's **abbreviate** what's left. First, we abbreviate "versus" to "v." following the examples in *The Bluebook*:

Southwest Engineering Company ~~and John Doe, Defendants-Appellants,~~ v. ~~The~~ United States ~~of America, Plaintiff-Appellee~~

Then, we look in T.6 to see which words in "Southwest Engineering Company" should be abbreviated. Notice that T.6 abbreviates "Southwest" as "Sw." Next, we notice that both "Engineering" and "Company" are listed in T.6; so we abbreviate those words:

Sw. Eng'g Co. ~~and John Doe, Defendants-Appellants,~~ v. ~~The~~ United States ~~of America, Plaintiff-Appellee~~

Finally, we know that Rule 10.2.2 says not to abbreviate "United States." So, all we have to do is italicize the case name, and it's ready to take its place in a citation sentence!

*Sw. Eng'g Co. v. United States*

But what if we wanted to use this case name in a *textual* sentence? Rule 10.2.1(c) tells us that, in a textual sentence, we only abbreviate the words in a case name that are listed in 10.2.1(c) regardless of whether the words are listed in T.6. Neither "Southwest" nor "Engineering" is on the 10.2.1(c) "short list." However, "Company" is. Therefore, if we wanted to use this case name in a textual sentence, it would look like this:

*Southwest Engineering Co. v. United States*

## Checklist for Case Names

- Have you italicized the case name?
- Have you omitted all words required by 10.2.1?
    - additional parties or actions (10.2.1(a))
    - procedural phrases (10.2.1(b))
    - "The" (10.2.1(d))
    - descriptive terms (10.2.1(e))
    - geographical terms (10.2.1(f)) except when part of a business name
    - given names or initials of individuals (10.2.1(g))
    - business firm designations if other words indicate a business (10.2.1(h))
- Have you abbreviated as necessary?
    - words in 10.2.1(c)
    - words in T.6
    - words in T.10 unless the unit is a named party
    - party names usually referred to by commonly-known initials (10.2.1(c))
- Have you *not* abbreviated as necessary?
    - geographical units named as parties
    - "United States"
    - all words other than those in 10.2.1(c) if your citation is in a textual rather than citation sentence

## Exercise 1
## Case Names

Put the following case name information in correct *Bluebook* citation form. All cases are being cited in citation sentences unless the problem indicates otherwise. This exercise focuses on Rules 10.2.1 and 10.2.2, B13, and T.6.

**Before beginning online exercises, complete the online intro quiz.**

**1.** Mary T. Akootchook versus The United States of America

______________________________

______________________________

**2.** Union Pacific Railroad Company versus Lloyd's of London

______________________________

______________________________

**3.** A Utah Supreme Court case, The State of Utah, Plaintiff-Appellant, versus Gabriel Valenzuela, Defendant-Appellee

______________________________

______________________________

**4.** St. Paul Fire & Marine Insurance Company, Plaintiff and Appellant, versus The First Bank of Arkansas, Defendant and Appellee

______________________________

______________________________

**5.** A single action styled Florida Web Printing v. Impact Advertising, Impact Advertising v. Florida Web Printing

______________________________

______________________________

**6.** In the matter of Karla R., et al., Persons Coming Under the Juvenile Court Law

______________________________

______________________________

**7.** Citizens for Honest and Responsible Government, Appellant, v. Dean Heller, Secretary of State of Nevada

______________________________

______________________________

**8.** Federal Communications Commission, Petitioner, v. National Citizens Committee for Broadcasting, Respondent [Note: The Federal Communications Commission is commonly referred to by its initials, FCC.]

______________________________

______________________________

**9.** The Estate of Elvis Presley

______________________________

______________________________

**10.** Mary Adkisson, Appellant, v. Git-n-Go Convenience Stores, Appellee

______________________________________________

______________________________________________

**11.** Catherine M. and Leonard C. Hoste, Plaintiff-Appellant, v. Radio Corporation of America Record Sales, Defendant-Appellee [Note: Radio Corporation of America is commonly referred to by its initials, RCA.]

______________________________________________

______________________________________________

**12.** In a brief to a Texas state court, cite P.A.B. on behalf of V.B., versus the State of Florida, a Florida Supreme Court case.

______________________________________________

______________________________________________

**13.** Roger L. McClung, et al., Plaintiffs-Appellants, v. Wal-Mart Stores, Incorporated, Defendant-Appellee

______________________________________________

______________________________________________

**14.** David Juliano, Plaintiff-Appellant-Respondent, v. Prudential Securities Incorporated, Defendant-Respondent-Appellant, and Forest Electric Corp., Defendant-Respondent

______________________________________________

______________________________________________

**15.** Joseph Smith, Bessie Smith, Francesca Smith and Angelus Williams, Plaintiffs-Appellees, versus Officer Victor Jones and Officer Shontae Jennings, each in their individual and official capacities, Defendants-Appellants

______________________________________________

______________________________________________

# Chapter 2
# CASE LOCATION

Now that you know how to begin your legal case citation with the proper case name, you are ready to tackle the second major part of the citation: the case location information. Currently, the most commonly used location information for a case is the case's location in a reporter. In that case, the citation "formula" is one you are already familiar with:

*Party 1 v. Party 2*, **Vol. Reporter Pg.** (Court Date)

However, some jurisdictions have adopted location information that references the year of the decision and a number assigned to the case by the court that issued the opinion. That citation format is called "public domain format." Citations using public domain format use this formula:

*Party 1 v. Party 2*, **Year STATE No.**

You may or may not be able to tell that the comma following the case name in each formula is not italicized. Rule 2.1(f) tells us to italicize commas that are *within* italicized material but not those that *follow* italicized material. Because the comma after a case name follows italicized material, it is not italicized.

*The Bluebook* quick reference for the case location in a citation is B5.1.2 of the Bluepages. Review this on page 7 of *The Bluebook* before continuing with this chapter.

### A. Reporters

A "reporter" is a compilation of judicial opinions, or cases. The compilation may be by jurisdiction (*e.g.*, *Florida Reports*) or by subject matter (*e.g.*, *Education Law Reporter*). A given case will be published in the reporter or reporters for that case's jurisdiction and may also appear in a subject matter reporter that contains other cases with the same topic. Legal citation, however, references only jurisdictional reporters.

Jurisdictional reporters may be either official publications of the state or federal government or unofficial publications of private publishers. Both official and unofficial reporters are printed in series. Generally, reporter publishers will begin a new series rather than allow the volume numbers to exceed three digits. Therefore, after volume 999 of *South Western Reporter*, Second Series, the publisher next published volume 1 of *South Western Reporter*, Third Series.

State court cases are published in both state and regional reporters. State reporters may be official or unofficial and contain cases from only one state. Regional reporters are unofficial reporters published by West Group. These reporters contain state court cases from several states. For example, *Southern Reporter* publishes state court cases from Alabama, Florida, Louisiana, and Mississippi.

Federal cases are published in jurisdictional reporters by level of court. Federal district court cases are published in *Federal Supplement*. Federal courts of appeals cases are published in *Federal Reporter*. United States Supreme Court cases are published in three reporters: *United States Reports* (official), *Supreme Court Reporter* (unofficial), and *Lawyers' Edition* (unofficial).

Rule 10.3.2 tells us that a citation must include a volume designation, the abbreviated name of the reporter, and the page on which the opinion begins in the reporter. Table 1 (T.1) of *The Bluebook* is a listing of information for each jurisdiction in the United States. The listing first gives federal information and then state information organized alphabetically by state name. The first information given for each jurisdiction is the names of the courts in that jurisdiction, the names of the reporters for each court, and the abbreviations for those reporters.

Placing the volume designation in the citation is straightforward. The volume number appears on the spine of the reporter, and that number is the first information given in the case location portion of the citation.

Placing the reporter information in the citation requires a little more information. The abbreviation for the reporter is in the appropriate jurisdictional section of T.1. [1] Pay special attention to the spacing of the abbreviation. This spacing follows the rules given in 6.1(a). Rule 6.1(a) tells us to close up adjacent single capitals (*e.g.*, N.Y.). Ordinals (*e.g.*, 1st, 2d, 4th, etc.) are treated as single capitals (*e.g.*, S.W.2d). Longer abbreviations and single capitals adjacent to longer abbreviations should have a space between them (*e.g.*, Ala.^App. and F.^Supp.). [2] You can combine these spacing rules to handle both adjacent single capitals and longer abbreviations in the same reporter abbreviation (*e.g.*, N.C.^Ct.^App.).

Finally, the number of the first page that the case appears on in the reporter follows the reporter abbreviation. When you give the reader the initial page number of the case, he or she has the information needed to find the case.

*Hunter v. Gatherer*, 789 Rptr. 234 (Ct. 2002).

Sometimes, you will also want to direct your reader's attention to specific material within the case. You can do this using a "pinpoint citation." Bluepages B5.1.2 says that you can pinpoint the location of specific information by following the initial page number in the citation with a comma, a space, and the page number containing the specific material. This specific page number is included *in addition to* the initial page number rather than as a substitute for it.

*Hunter v. Gatherer*, 789 Rptr. 234, 237 (Ct. 2002).

If your pinpointed material spans more than one page, B5.1.2 tells you to give the beginning and ending page numbers, separated by a hyphen or dash.

*Tree v. Shrub*, 789 Rptr. 85, 87-89 (Ct. 2002).

If the page numbers contain more than two digits, you should drop repetitious digits but always retain the last two digits.

*Hunter v. Gatherer*, 789 Rptr. 234, 237–39 (Ct. 2002).

Let's try an example to see how these rules work together. Say we have a Louisiana case called *Red v. Green. Red v. Green* is published in the Second Series of the *Southern Reporter*, volume 999, beginning on page 111. First, we know that the volume number goes first. It follows immediately after the case name, separated by a comma and a single space.

*Red v. Green*, 999

Next comes the reporter. It has to be abbreviated, so we look under the jurisdiction of the case, "Louisiana," in T.1 and find that *Southern Reporter* is

[1] *The Bluebook* contains a typographical error that is potentially confusing. You may want to note this correction in your copy. In T.1. in the federal section listing for "District Courts," the first reporter listed is "Federal Supplement." The abbreviation given for the second series of this reporter should include a period following "Supp."

[2] The caret symbol (^) in these examples shows the location of the space but would not actually be included in your citation.

abbreviated "So." or "So. 2d," depending on whether the case is printed in the First or Second Series. We know that our volume is in the Second Series, so "So. 2d" it is. Now we check Rule 6.1(a) to see the proper spacing to use in the abbreviation. "So." is a longer abbreviation, and "2d" is an ordinal considered as a single capital. In that case, 6.1(a) tells us to put a space between them.

*Red v. Green*, 999 So. 2d

In many reporters, the header of each page contains a notation that reads "Cite as:" followed by the volume, reporter abbreviation, and page number of the case. While we can rely on the given volume and page number, be careful about relying on that header for the reporter abbreviation. The spacing in those abbreviations does not always conform to *The Bluebook*. For example, West's *Federal Supplement* headers give "F.Supp." as the appropriate abbreviation. However, Rule 6.1(a) requires a space between "F." and "Supp."

Back to our citation: All we lack is the beginning page number of the case. After we add that, the name and reporter elements of our citation are as follows:

*Red v. Green*, 999 So. 2d 111

If we were citing to specific pages, 115 through 116, for example, in *Red v. Green*, they would follow the first page of the case. Remember, according to B5.1.2, we add the specific pinpoint reference to our citation after the page on which our case begins. Remember that when a pinpoint reference includes a span of pages, the first and last page of the span should be joined with a hyphen or dash. This page span contains repetitious digits (the "11" in 115 and 116), so this will invoke the rule that any repetitious digits except for the last two should be dropped. Therefore, the first "1" would be dropped because it is a repetitious digit. The second "1" would be retained because, even though it is a repetitious digit, it is also one of the last two digits. Then the name and reporter elements of our citation would be this:

*Red v. Green*, 999 So. 2d 111, 115–16

## B. Public Domain Format

Rule 10.3.3 provides an alternative to reporter citations. This alternative is called "public domain format." Public domain format allows citation to the year of the decision, the state's two-letter postal code, the court's abbreviation from Table 7 (T.7) if the court is not the highest court in the state, and the sequential number of the decision as assigned by the court issuing the opinion.

*Party 1 v. Party 2*, **Year STATE No.**

Although this is the formula adopted by many states and suggested by Rule 10.3.3, individual states may adopt a different public domain format. In that case, we follow that state's local rules for its public domain format.

When a citation to a regional reporter is available, Rule 10.3.3 requires public domain format *in addition to* a reporter citation. Otherwise, public domain format is used alone, without a reporter citation. Just as when you cite to a reporter, you can pinpoint cite to specific material using public domain format. In that case, the pinpoint is to a paragraph rather than a page. To determine whether a state requires citation using public domain format, consult that jurisdiction's information in T.1.

Drafting public domain format is pretty simple. Let's say you want to cite *Orange v. Purple*, a North Dakota case decided in 2004. This was the ninety-sixth case decided in 2004 by the North Dakota Court of Appeals. The case is not included in *North Western Reporter*, the regional reporter that includes North Dakota state cases.

First, we look in T.1 under "North Dakota" to see if North Dakota has adopted a public domain format. We find that, for cases decided after January 1, 1997, North Dakota has adopted the public domain format suggested by Rule 10.3.3. Therefore, we start with the year of decision:

*Orange v. Purple*, 2004

Next, we add the two-letter postal code for North Dakota (ND).

*Orange v. Purple*, 2004 ND

Because this case was not decided by the highest court in the state, we will also need an abbreviation for the court. We turn to T.7 and find that the abbreviation for a state "Court of Appeals" is "Ct. App." Because "Ct." and "App." are longer abbreviations under Rule 6.1(a), we will place a space between them.

*Orange v. Purple*, 2004 ND Ct. App.

Finally, we add the sequential number of the decision, 96. Because we do not need any more information to make this citation complete, we can place a period at the end of our citation sentence. Notice that this differs from reporter citations in that reporter citations require a court and date parenthetical before they are complete. (Chapter 3 introduces you to the court and date parenthetical.)

*Orange v. Purple*, 2004 ND Ct. App. 96.

If you wanted to direct your reader's attention to specific material, you could use a pinpoint. Remember that public domain cites pinpoint information by paragraph rather than by page. Therefore, if the information you wanted to point out is found in the eleventh paragraph of the opinion, you would pinpoint this way:

*Orange v. Purple*, 2004 ND Ct. App. 96, ¶ 11.

## Checklist for Print Reporters

- Have you put the volume number first?
- Have you abbreviated the reporter name as shown in T.1?
- Have you closed up adjacent single capitals as shown in Rule 6.1(a)?
- Have you given the first page of the case, even if there is also a pinpoint citation?
- Have you checked to make sure you have not put an extra space anywhere?

## Checklist for Public Domain Format

- Have you consulted T.1 to see if the case's jurisdiction has adopted a public domain format? If it has, continue. If it has not, give a citation to a reporter rather than public domain format.
- Have you put the year of decision first?
- Have you given the state's two-letter postal code?
- If the case is not from the highest court in the state, have you added the abbreviation from T.7 for the court? If so, have you closed up adjacent single capitals as shown in Rule 6.1(a)?
- Have you given the sequential number of the decision?
- If you need to direct your reader to specific material, have you included a pinpoint to the paragraph containing the material?
- Have you placed a period at the end of the citation?

## Exercise 2
## Case Location

Put the following case name information and reporter or public domain information in correct *Bluebook* citation form. Do not put a period at the conclusion of the "citation" you draft if a court and date parenthetical would be needed to complete the citation. All cases are being cited in citation sentences in a brief to be filed with the United States Supreme Court. Although this exercise builds on the rules used in the previous exercise, this exercise focuses on B5.1.2 and Rules 10.3.2, 10.3.3, 3.2, 3.3, and 6.1(a). You will also need to refer to T.1 for information on reporter abbreviations and public domain format. If no public domain information is given, assume that none is available.

1. Ernesto A. Miranda, Petitioner, versus the State of Arizona. This is a United States Supreme Court case reported in volume 384, page 436, of *United States Reports.*

______________________________________________

______________________________________________

2. Robert S. Minnick, Petitioner, versus the State of Mississippi, Respondent. This is a Supreme Court of Mississippi case reported in volume 551, page 77, of *Southern Reporter*, Second Series. You wish to direct your reader's attention to specific material appearing on page 79.

______________________________________________

______________________________________________

3. Montana Chamber of Commerce versus Ed Argenbright and League of Women Voters of Montana. This is a United States Court of Appeals case reported in volume 226, page 1049, of *Federal Reporter*, Third Series.

______________________________________________

______________________________________________

4. TS 1 Partnership and John Sletten, Plaintiffs-Appellee, versus Penny Allred, d/b/a It's About Time, Defendant-Appellant. This is a Utah Court of Appeals case reported in volume 877, page 156, of *Pacific Reporter*, Second Series.

______________________________________________

______________________________________________

5. Ronald Hart, on behalf of himself and all others similarly situated, Plaintiff, v. Internet Wire, Incorporated, and Bloomberg, L.P., Defendants This is a United States District Court case reported in volume 163, page 316 of *Federal Supplement*, Second Series. You wish to direct your reader's attention to specific material found on page 319 of volume 163.

______________________________________________

______________________________________________

6. Paul Smith versus Dr. Marc Harr and Central Florida Distributing Company. This is a Florida District Court of Appeals, Fifth District, case reported in volume 570, page 575, of *Southern Reporter*, Second Series.

______________________________________________

______________________________________________

7. John W. Carson, d/b/a Johnny Carson and Johnny Carson, Apparel, Inc., Plaintiffs, v. Here's Johnny Portable Toilets, Incorporated, Defendant. This is a United States District Court case reported in volume 498, page 71, of *Federal Supplement.*

______________________________________________

______________________________________________

8. Ann Lukas, Appellant, v. Saint Francis Hospital and Medical Center, Neurosurgical Associates, Inc., and Joseph Sadowski, a neurosurgeon, Appellees. This is a Connecticut Appellate Court case reported in volume 583, page 941, of *Atlantic Reporter*, Second Series.

______________________________________________

______________________________________________

9. Mark E. Towner, Petitioner and Appellee v. Michael Ridgway, Respondent and Appellant. This is a Supreme Court of Utah opinion issued as the 23rd opinion of 2008 and filed on March 4, 2008. You may assume that no reporter information is currently available for this case.

______________________________________________

______________________________________________

10. Ryan Koble Plaintiff and Appellee v. Jamie Koble, Defendant and Appellant. This is a Supreme Court of North Dakota opinion issued as the 11th opinion of 2008 and filed on January 17, 2008. You wish to direct your reader's attention to specific material in paragraph 1 of the opinion. Assume that no reporter information is available for this case.

______________________________________________

______________________________________________

# Chapter 3
# COURT & DATE

Congratulations! Now that you have mastered two major parts of a basic case citation, case names and case locations, you are ready to learn the third and final portion of a case citation: the parenthetical containing the court deciding the case and the year of that decision. The court and date parenthetical appears immediately following the page information in your case citation. Now that you have constructed a full citation, you should end it with a period. A case citation used as a citation sentence, *i.e.*, not embedded in a textual sentence, should be punctuated as a sentence: Begin with a capital letter and end by placing a period after the court and date parenthetical. The general rules concerning this portion of the citation are B5.1.3 in the Bluepages, and Rules 10.4 and 10.5, so you should read these rules carefully before attempting Exercise 3.

*Party 1 v. Party 2*, Vol. Reporter Pg. **(Court Date)**.

*The Bluebook* quick reference for the court and date is B5.1.3 of the Bluepages.

## A. Court Information

By looking at a case citation, your reader should be able to determine what court decided the case. Generally, Rule B5.1.3 requires that a legal writer indicate both the name of the state and the name of the court of decision in the court and date parenthetical. Therefore, the court of appeals in Minnesota becomes "Minn. Ct. App." However, some exceptions apply. You omit the name of the court if the court is the highest court in the jurisdiction. This rule is consistent with the abbreviations of state supreme courts, *i.e.*, "Tex." and "Mass." In addition, you omit the jurisdiction information if the title of the reporter unambiguously gives that information to the reader. For example, *United States Reports* publishes only cases decided by the United States Supreme Court. Therefore, a cite to a case published in *United States Reports* can refer only to a United States Supreme Court case. Therefore, you would not include additional information in the court and date parenthetical.

*Boerne v. Flores*, 521 U.S. 507 (1997).

### 1. State Cases

Some states have official reporters that publish only cases decided by that state's highest court. For those citations, as mentioned above, Rule B5.1.3 provides that no additional information in the court and date parenthetical is necessary. For example, *South Dakota Reports* publishes only cases decided by the South Dakota Supreme Court, and the South Dakota Supreme Court is the highest court in the jurisdiction. Therefore, a cite to a case published in *South Dakota Reports* would not include additional information in the court and date parenthetical.

*Landrum v. DeBruycker*, 90 S.D. 304, 240 N.W.2d 119 (1976).

However, most reporters, particularly regional reporters, publish opinions from several different state courts. In each of those citations, you must include the jurisdiction and the name of the court that decided the case in question. T.1 lists the abbreviations for each state court. For example, if you have a case from the Montana Supreme Court, you can look in the Montana entry in T.1 and see that the abbreviation for that court appears in parentheses after the heading "Supreme Court" and only contains jurisdiction information: "Mont." The court information is not necessary because the court is the highest court in the jurisdiction. Because the reporter abbreviation "P.2d" does not indicate the jurisdiction that decided this case, you would include the entire abbreviation in the court and date parenthetical.

*State v. Ommundson*, 974 P.2d 620 (**Mont.** 1999).

Similarly, the *North Western Reporter* publishes cases decided by the highest and intermediate courts in seven different states. Therefore, if you are citing a Michigan Court of Appeals case and are citing to *North Western Reporter*, you would convey both the jurisdiction and court information to your reader in the court and date parenthetical. You would use the proper abbreviation for the Michigan Court of Appeals that is given in T.1 in the parentheses following the heading "Court of Appeals": "Mich. Ct. App." Because the court is only an intermediate appellate court, you must include both jurisdiction and court information. (We will discuss when a writer needs to cite to a regional reporter and an official state reporter in connection with Exercise 4, Parallel Citations.)

*Rutherford v. Chrysler Motors Corp.*, 231 N.W.2d 413 (**Mich. Ct. App.** 1975).

But wait, there's more! *The Bluebook* adds another twist in B.5.1.3(v) and Rule 10.4(b). Some states publish an official reporter for cases from more than a single court, *e.g.*, from the supreme court and the appellate courts. Other states have special reporters for just intermediate or trial courts. If the name of the reporter tells your reader the name of the state, then you omit the state information from the court and date parenthetical because it's not necessary; however, you still include the court abbreviation in the court and date parenthetical. For example, if you were going to cite to a New Mexico Court of Appeals case that was reported in *New Mexico Reports*, which publishes cases from different courts, but only courts in New Mexico, then you should omit the "N.M." portion of the correct abbreviation "N.M. Ct. App."

*Lara v. City of Albuquerque*, 126 N.M. 455, 921 P.2d 846 (**Ct. App.** 1998).

As you might guess, you have citations like the above example only in certain states; this situation occurs only when you have an official state reporter in addition to the regional reporter.

### 2. Federal Cases

You must designate a court when citing to any federal case other than a Supreme Court case. The *Federal Reporter* publishes cases from each of the federal courts of appeals. The *Federal Supplement* publishes cases from each United States district court. If you have a case reported in the *Federal Reporter*, you can look under "United States Jurisdictions — Federal" in T.1 and find the heading "Courts of Appeals" or "Jurisdiction-Specific Citation Rules and Style Guides" in BT.2. You will see in parentheses after that heading that you must tell your reader which court of appeals decided the case by using the proper abbreviation for that court. The parenthetical provides you with an example. The Court of Appeals for the Second Circuit is abbreviated "2d Cir." Using that example and the table at BT.2 as a guideline, you can formulate the proper abbreviations for each of the circuit courts of appeals: 1st, 2d, 3d, 4th, 5th, 6th, 7th, 8th, 9th, 10th, and 11th. The federal circuit court that sits in the District of Columbia is abbreviated "D.C. Cir."

*Deus v. Allstate Ins. Co.*, 15 F.3d 506 (**5th Cir.** 1994).

Pay particular attention to cases decided by the Fifth Circuit in 1981 and 1982. The Fifth Circuit split into the Fifth and Eleventh Circuits on October 1, 1981. Rule 10.8.2 will give you guidance on whether you need additional information in your court and date parenthetical to indicate a case decided during the split.

If you have a case reported in the *Federal Supplement*, you should look under the heading "Federal Courts" in the federal jurisdiction section of BT.2. Using the listings of court rules for each court, you can form the abbreviation for all the U.S. district courts. The abbreviation for a district court is "D." To that you will always add the state in which the court sits (*e.g.* D. **Mass.**). If that state contains more than one federal district, an additional abbreviation is included prior to "D." (*e.g.*, "**S.**D. Tex." for the Southern District of Texas). Just remember that, according to Rule 6.1(a), adjacent capitals do not have spaces between them (S.D.N.Y.), but you must put a space between capitals and other abbreviations (D. Mass.).

*Jones v. Clinton*, 57 F. Supp. 2d 719 (**E.D. Ark.** 1999).

Bottom line: Your reader must be able to tell what court in what jurisdiction decided a certain case by looking at the citation. Whatever information the reporter does not give, you must include in the court and date parenthetical.

**B. Date Information**

Your reader also must be able to glean from your citation the date that your case was decided. Please note that the important date is the date the case was *decided*, not the date the case was *argued* or *heard*. For the majority of the cases that you cite, you will know what year the case was decided from reading the heading of the case in a reporter. For these cases, you simply include the year in the court and date parenthetical.

*Stein v. Plainwell Cmty. Schs.*, 822 F.2d 1406 (6th Cir. **1987**).

Again, watch for cases decided by the Fifth Circuit during the 1981 split. Rule 10.8.2 tells us that for cases decided in 1981, you must also include the month along with the year of decision. (Note that T.12 provides the proper abbreviations of the months of the year.)

Also, for cases that are not published in a reporter, you will need to include additional information other than the year of decision, according to Rule 18.1.1. For instance, if a case is not reported or is reported in a slip opinion or an electronic database, then you must give the exact date, *i.e.*, month, day, and year, of the decision.

*Williams v. State*, 2002 WL 243589 (Ark. Feb. 21, 2002).

## Checklist for Court Information

- Are you citing from a federal reporter, a regional reporter, or a state reporter?
- If a federal reporter, but not *United States Reports*, have you included an abbreviation for the deciding court as shown in BT.2?
- If a regional reporter, have you included a full abbreviation for the deciding court as shown in T.1?
- If a state reporter, have you included an abbreviation for the deciding court, as shown in T.1, but not the abbreviation for the state?
- Have you double-checked the spacing of your abbreviation according to Rule 6.1(a)?

## Checklist for Date Information

- Is your case published in a reporter? If so, have you included the year of decision in your citation?
- If your case is not reported in print, have you included the month, day, and year in your citation?

## Exercise 3
## Court & Date

Put the following information in correct *Bluebook* form. All cases are being cited in citation sentences. Although this exercise builds on the rules used in the previous exercise, this exercise focuses on Rules 10.4 and 10.5. You will also need to refer to T.1 for information on the reporters containing cases from the appropriate jurisdiction. For each question, you must use the correct typeface given in B13 and the correct spacing given in Rule 6.1(a).

**1.** Julie A. Else versus Timothy L. Else, a case from the Court of Appeals of Nebraska, decided January 14, 1997, and reported at volume 558, page 594, of the *North Western Reporter*, Second Series.

______________________________________________

______________________________________________

**2.** The United States of America versus Eddie Wayne Roberson, a case from the United States Court of Appeals, Fifth Circuit, decided April 28, 1989, and reported at volume 872, page 597, of *Federal Reporter*, Second Series.

______________________________________________

______________________________________________

**3.** Rothman Realty Corp. versus Barton Bereck and Debra Bereck, his wife, a case from the Superior Court of New Jersey, Appellate Division, decided March 17, 1976, and reported at volume 355, page 201, of *Atlantic Reporter*, Second Series.

______________________________________________

______________________________________________

**4.** Karen Derby versus The Connecticut Light and Power Company, a case from the Supreme Court of Connecticut, decided August 20, 1974, and reported at volume 355, page 244, of *Atlantic Reporter*, Second Series.

______________________________________________

______________________________________________

**5.** Harland Macia, III, d/b/a Catamount Software, versus Microsoft Corporation, Intuit, Inc., and Meca Software, LLC, a case from the United States District Court of the District of Vermont, decided on June 21, 2001, and reported at volume 152, page 535, of *Federal Supplement*, Second Series.

______________________________________________

______________________________________________

**6.** Southern California Edison Company versus Public Utilities Commission, a case decided by the California Court of Appeal, Second District, Division 3, on December 29, 2000, and reported at volume 85, page 1086, of *California Appellate Reports*, Fourth Series.

______________________________________________

______________________________________________

**7.** Albert Henri Diremiggio versus the State of Texas, a case from the Court of Criminal Appeals of Texas, decided July 7, 1982, and reported at volume 637, page 926, of *South Western Reporter*, Second Series.

______________________________________________

______________________________________________

**8.** Twentieth Century Fox Film Corporation versus Marvel Enterprises, Inc., et al., a case from the United States District Court for the Southern District of New York, decided on August 9, 2001, and reported at volume 155, page 1, of *Federal Supplement*, Second Series.

______________________________________________

______________________________________________

**9.** The People of the State of New York versus Alvin Weiss, a/k/a Mark Glass, a case from the New York Supreme Court, Appellate Division, decided on February 26, 1998, and reported at volume 671, page 604, of *New York Supplement*, Second Series.

______________________________________________

______________________________________________

**10.** Republic Insurance Company, a Texas corporation, and Vanguard Insurance Company, a Texas corporation, Plaintiffs-Appellants, versus Honorable Millard H. Oakley, Commissioner of Insurance of the State of Tennessee, Defendant-Appellee, a case from the Supreme Court of Tennessee, decided May 17, 1982, and reported at volume 637, page 448, of *South Western Reporter*, Second Series.

______________________________________________

______________________________________________

# Chapter 4
# PARALLEL CITATIONS

Now that you have mastered the basic citation, you are ready to add a twist. The first thing we will add is the parallel citation. A parallel citation is one that contains location information for more than one source of the case.

*Fence v. Post*, 111 St. Rptr. 222, 888 Reg. Rptr. 999 (2001).

*The Bluebook* quick reference for the parallel citation is in B5.1.3 at the bottom third of page 9. Read this before continuing with this chapter.

You learned from the previous exercises that some states have their opinions published in their own state reporter as well as the appropriate regional reporter. For example, opinions from the Idaho Supreme Court and the Idaho Court of Appeals are published in both *Idaho Reports* and *Pacific Reporter*. When you cite opinions from such a state to a court in that state, and when local rules of citation require it, B5.1.3 and Rule 10.3.1 tell you to give a citation to both the state and regional reporters. Remember also that some states have adopted a public domain format according to Rule 10.3.3 for citations to that state's opinions. When citing to decisions from those states to those states' courts, Rule 10.3.3 requires a citation to both the public domain information and the regional reporter information.

However, if you are citing in a document to be filed with a federal court or a court outside the state in which the case was decided, you will cite to only the regional reporter. Before you begin the Parallel Citations exercise, read Rules 10.3.1 and 10.3.3 carefully.

The first decision you have to make is whether you need a parallel citation. If your case is from a federal court, you will not parallel cite. This rule extends to United States Supreme Court cases as well. Even though they are published in *United States Reports, Supreme Court Reporter,* and *Lawyers' Edition*, T.1 tells you to cite to only *United States Reports.*

### A. States Not Requiring Public Domain Format

If your case is from a state that has its own reporter and you are citing this case in a document to a state court in that state, you will *usually* cite both the state and the regional reporters. You should consult local rules or customs to determine whether you should cite both the state and regional reporters. BT.2 will help you find jurisdiction- specific rules of citation. If you do cite both the state and regional reporters, you will use T.1 in much the same way you do for any citation.

First, determine the jurisdiction of the case. Next, look up that jurisdiction in T.1. Table 1 will tell you which reporters to cite and how those reporters are abbreviated. You see from the bottom of page 9 of *The Bluebook* that the state reporter is listed first in a parallel citation, and the regional reporter should be listed second. Remember that some cases are printed in many different sources besides just state and regional reporters. Some publishers print subject matter reporters, compiling all the opinions in a certain subject area into one reporter. Also, some secondary research sources, such as *American Law Reports* (A.L.R.), publish the full text of opinions related to the articles they publish. Regardless of the number of publications in which your case is published, you will only cite to the reporters listed in T.1. [1]

The next decision with a parallel citation is whether and how to identify the jurisdiction and name of the court that issued the opinion. Remember that the general rule, according to Rule 10.4(b), is that you include both the state's abbreviation (*e.g.*, N.M.) and the name of the court (*e.g.*, Ct. App.). The abbreviations for the states can be found in T.10 or in that state's section of T.1. The abbreviations for the court can be found in T.7 or in that court's subsection within its state section in T.1. The first exception to 10.4(b)'s general rule is that you need not include the name of the court if the court of decision is the highest court of the state. So if your case is from the highest court in the state, omit the name of the court, and your reader will assume that the case is from the highest court in the state.

*W. Edmond Salt Water Disposal Ass'n v. Rosecrans*, 226 P.2d 965 (**Okla.** 1950).

The second exception is that you need not include the state abbreviation if it is obvious from the name of the reporter.

*Lukowsky v. Shalit*, 487 N.Y.S.2d 781 (**App. Div.** 1985).

Remembering these rules might be easier if you know the rationale behind them. The basic rationale behind every citation rule is to keep the citation as short as possible while still conveying all significant information. This is why we include only the state and regional reporter and not every possible source that might publish an opinion. Also for the sake of brevity, we assume that the court is the highest court in the state unless the citation tells us otherwise. [2] Likewise, why include the state abbreviation if it is obvious from the name of the reporter? Wait a minute . . . if brevity is so important, then why use a parallel citation at all? The answer is "convenience." Some practitioners and courts will subscribe only to the state reporter, usually because of financial or shelf-space constraints. A parallel citation helps people using only the state reporter from having to resort to a cross-reference index each time they want to look up a case.

Let's try an example to see how these rules work. Suppose you want to cite the Georgia Supreme Court case *Black v. Blue* in a brief you will file with the Georgia Court of Appeals. This is a 1972 case that is reported at volume 321, page 543, of *Georgia Reports*, Georgia's state reporter. This opinion is also reported at volume 76, page 123, of *South Eastern Reporter*, Second Series. *South Eastern Reporter* is the regional reporter that includes Georgia state cases.

Let's get the easy part of the citation out of the way first. We know we can start with the case name:

*Black v. Blue*,

Now, let's tackle the first decision: whether to include a parallel citation. This is a Georgia case, and we will be citing it to a Georgia court. Because we are citing a

---

[1] Do not be fooled by citations you read in reported cases! For example, opinions published in the West regional reporter system often contain parallel citations to other subject matter reporters published by West. These types of parallel citations do not conform to *The Bluebook* and should not be copied into your own writing.

[2] Did you realize that citation form and legal ethics are intertwined? Opinions from the highest court in the state have greater authority than lower court opinions. If you do not include the abbreviation for a lower court in a citation to a lower court opinion, not only is your citation incorrect, but you may also be representing to the court that your case has greater authority than it does.

Georgia case to a Georgia court, this case meets the first criterion for a parallel citation. The next criterion is whether Georgia local rules actually require a parallel citation. Assume that you have consulted the local rules for Georgia, and those rules indicate the need for a parallel citation to the state and regional reporters.

Because this is a Georgia case, we will go to the section for Georgia in T.1. Our case is from the Georgia Supreme Court, so we will be using the first part of this section. This section tells us that *Georgia Reports* is the state reporter for Georgia (and we see also that "Ga." is the abbreviation for *Georgia Reports*) and that S.E.2d is the regional reporter for Georgia cases (we see that "S.E.2d" is the abbreviation for *South Eastern Reporter*, Second Series). This section contains the information we'll need for a parallel citation. It tells us that (1) the reporters we should cite to are *Georgia Reports* and *South Eastern Reporter*, (2) the abbreviations for those reporters are Ga. and S.E.2d, and (3) if the opinion is not in S.E.2d, a citation to Ga. will be sufficient.

Remember that we follow the examples in *The Bluebook* and list the state reporter before the regional reporter. Finally, Rule 10.3.1(b) tells us that if we do not need a parallel cite, *i.e.*, we are not citing a Georgia case to a Georgia court, then we would only cite to *South Eastern Reporter*. Whew! Let's put that information to work:

*Black v. Blue*, 321 Ga. 543, 76 S.E.2d 123

Now, let's tackle our next decision: how and whether to identify the state in the court and date parenthetical. Rule 10.4(b) tells us that we do not name the court (*e.g.*, Ct. App.) if it is the highest court in the state. In looking at the Georgia section in T.1, we see that the Supreme Court is the highest court in Georgia. Therefore, we will not need to name the court. Further, because the name of the state is obvious from the name of one of the reporters (Ga.), we do not include the state abbreviation. So the only information left to include in the citation is the year of the decision, 1972, and a period ends our citation sentence.

*Black v. Blue*, 321 Ga. 543, 76 S.E.2d 123 (1972).

Got it? Okay, now take a deep breath, and let's try the same citation in a court document filed with a federal court or a state court outside of Georgia (the rules are the same for both). Rule 10.3.1(b) tells you to cite the regional reporter in this situation, so start with the *South Eastern Reporter* information.

*Black v. Blue*, 76 S.E.2d 123

Next, decide how and whether to identify the court and jurisdiction in the court and date parenthetical. We are still dealing with the highest court in the state, so we still do not include a court name. However, now the jurisdiction is not obvious from the name of the reporter. *South Eastern Reporter* publishes cases from many states. So we will need to include the abbreviation for the state.

*Black v. Blue*, 76 S.E.2d 123 (Ga.

Finish it off with the year of decision and a period at the end of our citation sentence, and we are done!

*Black v. Blue*, 76 S.E.2d 123 (Ga. 1972).

### B. States Requiring Public Domain Format

Remember from Chapter 2 that T.1 tells us which states require public domain format. So if you look up a state in T.1 and do not find a notation that the state has adopted public domain format, you should verify this online.

If a state does require public domain format, Rule 10.3.3 requires parallel citation to the public domain information and the regional reporter. However, if you give a parallel citation that includes public domain information, Rule 10.3.3 does not require a court and date parenthetical unless state local rules specifically call for one. The reason for omitting the parenthetical is that the information that would ordinarily be in that parenthetical — state abbreviation, court abbreviation, and year of decision — are all included in public domain format. Therefore, a court and date parenthetical is unnecessary.

Let's run through an example of a parallel citation that includes public domain format. Suppose we want to cite the North Dakota Supreme Court case *Apache Corp. v. MDU Res. Group, Inc.* This is a 1999 opinion that was issued as the 247th case by the court that year. The case is reported at volume 603, page 891 of *North Western Reporter*, Second Series. *North Western Reporter* is the regional reporter that includes North Dakota state cases.

The first decision is whether our citation should include public domain format. To find this out, we check North Dakota's section of T.1 and find that North Dakota has adopted the public domain format suggested by Rule 10.3.3. Therefore, we follow 10.3.3 and include both the public domain format and a citation to the regional reporter. Let's start with the public domain information. The first piece of information required is the year of decision.

*Apache Corp. v. MDU Res. Group, Inc.*, 1999

Next, we add the two-letter postal code for North Dakota. Because this case is from the highest court in the state, we do not include an abbreviation for the court name.

*Apache Corp. v. MDU Res. Group, Inc.*, 1999 ND

Finally, we add the sequential number of the case that was assigned by the court.

*Apache Corp. v. MDU Res. Group, Inc.*, 1999 ND 247

Now, let's add the citation for the regional reporter. We find the abbreviation for *North Western Reporter*, Second Series (N.W.2d), in the North Dakota section of T.1. Because the reporter abbreviation contains only adjacent single capitals, Rule 6.1(a) tells us to close up all letters in the abbreviation.

*Apache Corp. v. MDU Res. Group, Inc.*, 1999 ND 247, 603 N.W.2d 891

Because citations using the public domain format in Rule 10.3.3 do not require a court and date parenthetical, all we have to do is add a period to our citation sentence, and we're done!

*Apache Corp. v. MDU Res. Group, Inc.*, 1999 ND 247, 603 N.W.2d 891.

## Checklist for Parallel Citations

- Are you citing a state case?
  - If not, do not worry about parallel citation.
  - If so, are you citing the case to a state court in that same state?
    - If not, do not worry about parallel citation.
    - If so, turn to that state's section of T.1 to determine whether that state has adopted public domain format.
- If the state has **not** adopted public domain format . . .
  - have you used T.1 to determine which reporters to cite and how to abbreviate them?
  - have you listed state reporter(s) before the regional reporter?
  - have you included a state abbreviation in the court and date parenthetical only if the name of the state is not obvious from the reporter abbreviation?
  - have you included an abbreviation for the court only if the court is not the highest in the state?
- If the state **has** adopted public domain format . . .
  - have you listed the public domain information first?
  - have you included the citation to the regional reporter if one is available?
  - have you omitted the court and date parenthetical?
  - If the state has adopted a public domain format that differs from Rule 10.3.3, have you consulted local rules for the format and information to include?

## Exercise 4
## Parallel Citations

Put the following information in correct *Bluebook* citation form. All cases are being cited in citation sentences. Although this exercise builds on the rules used in previous exercises, this exercise focuses on Rule 10.3.1 and B5.1.3. You will also need to refer to T.1 for information on reporters containing cases in the appropriate jurisdiction and any required public domain format information. For each question, you must use the correct typeface given in B13 and the correct spacing given in Rule 6.1.

**1.** In a brief filed with a United States District Court, you cite the 1964 United States Supreme Court case Thomas D. George, et al., versus Douglas Aircraft Company, Incorporated. This case is reported in volume 379, page 904, of *United States Reports*; in volume 85, page 193, of *Supreme Court Reporter*; and in volume 13, page 177, of *Lawyers' Edition*, Second Series.

______________________________________________

______________________________________________

**2.** In a brief filed with the Ohio Court of Appeals, you cite the 2001 Ohio Supreme Court case John Andersen versus Highland House Company, et al., and Indiana Insurance Company. This case is reported in volume 757, page 329, of *North Eastern Reporter*, Second Series, and in volume 93, page 547, of *Ohio State Reports*, Third Series. Assume that the usual practice in Ohio is to cite to both the state and regional reporters.

______________________________________________

______________________________________________

**3.** In a brief filed with a United States Court of Appeals, you cite the 1983 Supreme Court of Connecticut case State of Connecticut v. James Young. The case is reported in volume 191, page 636, of *Connecticut Reports*, and in volume 469, page 1189, of *Atlantic Reporter*, Second Series.

______________________________________________

______________________________________________

**4.** In a brief filed with a Texas state district court, you cite the 1974 United States Supreme Court case United States versus Nicholas Giordano. The case is reported in volume 416, page 505, of *United States Reports*; in volume 94, page 1820, of *Supreme Court Reporter*; and in volume 40, page 341, of *Lawyers' Edition*, Second Series.

______________________________________________

______________________________________________

**5.** In a brief filed with the Supreme Court of Delaware, you cite the 1999 Maryland Court of Special Appeals case Judith A. Geduldig, et al., versus David B. Posner, et al. The case is reported in volume 129, page 490, of *Maryland Appellate Reports*, and in volume 743, page 247, of *Atlantic Reports*, Second Series.

______________________________________________

______________________________________________

**6.** In a brief filed with the United States Court of Appeals for the First Circuit, you cite the 1999 First Circuit case Henry John Fernandes, et al., Plaintiffs-Appellants, versus Costa Brothers Masonry, Incorporated, Defendant-Appellee. This case is reported in volume 81, page 1149, of *Fair Employment Practice Cases*, and in volume 199, page 572, of *Federal Reporter*, Third Series.

______________________________________________

______________________________________________

**7.** In a brief filed with an Arizona state trial court, you cite the 1945 Arizona Supreme Court case City of Tucson v. The Tucson Sunshine Climate Club. The case is reported in volume 64, page 1, of *Arizona Reports*, and in volume 164, page 598, of *Pacific Reporter*, Second Series. Assume that the usual practice in Arizona is to cite both state and regional reporters.

______________________________________________

______________________________________________

**8.** In a brief filed with a United States Court of Appeals, you cite the 1985 Michigan Court of Appeals case Lindsey Smith and Brenda Sanders, for themselves and for a class similarly situated, Plaintiffs-Appellants, versus The University of Detroit, a Michigan corporation. This case is reported in volume 145, page 468, of *Michigan Appeals Reports*; in volume 378, page 511, of *North Western Reporter*, Second Series; and in volume 29, page 384, of *Education Law Reports*.

______________________________________________

______________________________________________

**9.** In a brief filed with the Maine Supreme Judicial Court, you cite the 2007 Maine Supreme Judicial Court case Alan P. Hess versus Rhonda M. Hess. The case is reported in volume 927, page 391, of *Atlantic Reporter*, Second Series. This case was given the sequential number of 82 by the Maine Supreme Judicial Court.

______________________________________________

______________________________________________

**10.** In a brief filed with the South Dakota Supreme Court, you cite the 2007 South Dakota Supreme Court case Northland Insurance Company, Plaintiff and Appellant, versus Zurich American Insurance Company, Defendant and Appellee. The case is reported in volume 743, page 145, of *North Western Reporter*, Second Series. This case was given the sequential number of 126 by the South Dakota Supreme Court.

______________________________________________

______________________________________________

# Chapter 5
# SHORT FORMS (CASES)

Frequently, you will wish to refer to one case several times within a legal memorandum or a court document. Just to prove to you that *The Bluebook* does indeed have a heart, you need only to give the full legal citation for a case the *first* time that you cite to that case. For all subsequent cites to that case, you will use a short form citation, as long as all subsequent cites are within the same general discussion. Citing a case in full after having mentioned the case before will, in fact, confuse your reader. Your reader may think you are introducing a new case into your analysis. B5.2 and Rules 4.1 and 10.9 provide information on short form citations for cases. You should read each of those sections carefully before attempting Exercise 5.

The citation rules you have learned so far have required that you know only what source you are citing. However, the rules for short forms differ in that you must know not only what you are citing but also the context in which it is cited. Which short form you choose depends on the location of the short form in relation to previous citations to that and other sources.

*The Bluebook* provides two types of short forms to be used for cases in legal memoranda and court documents: "*id.*" and an abbreviated version of the full legal citation. These two types are not interchangeable, but can each be used only in certain instances. (Note that according to Rule 4.2, "*supra*" is not a permissible short form for certain frequently cited authorities, such as cases and statutes.)

Both B5.2 and Rule 4.1 explain the short form "*id.*" in detail and gives good examples. [1] The short form "*id.*" may only be used when you wish to cite to a case that is cited in the *immediately preceding citation*. In other words, no intervening cites to a different authority of any type should appear between the preceding citation to this case and the current citation. However, the preceding citation to the case may be a full citation or a short form citation, even another "*id.*" designation. Note, however, that simply mentioning a case name in a previous sentence will not support an "*id.*" citation. In addition, the prior citation need only be to the same case, not to the same page in the same case. If you wish to cite to the same page of the same case, then use only the word "*id.*" If you wish to cite to a different page or pages of the same case, include those page(s) immediately preceded by the word "at."

> Prior to being arrested, Mrs. Jones had accumulated over 100 speeding tickets. *State v. Jones*, 16 Rptr. 33, 34 (St. Ct. 1999). The majority of these tickets listed her speed as at least 20 miles per hour over the posted speed limit. *Id.* Five of the speeding tickets were issued in connection with traffic accidents. *Id.* at 35.

One more detail to remember: If the immediately preceding citation is a "string cite," *i.e.*, contains more than one authority, then you may not use "*id.*," even if one

---

[1] "Id." is an abbreviation for "idem," meaning "the same." It is not capitalized unless it begins a citation sentence. The period following the abbreviation is italicized, as provided in rule B13. In your earlier studies prior to law school, you may have used "ibid.," which is an abbreviation for the latin word "ibidem," which means "the same place." For whatever reason, legal writing has developed using only "id."

of those authorities is the case you currently wish to cite. Consider the following three cites that appear consecutively in a paragraph.

*State v. Jones*, 16 Rptr. 33, 34 (St. Ct. 1999).

*Id.*; *State v. Smith*, 19 Rptr. 389, 390-92 (St. Ct. 2002).

*Smith*, 19 Rptr. at 390-92.

The second citation is a string cite referring to both *Jones* and *Smith*. Because *Jones* was the immediately preceding citation, "*id.*" clearly refers to that case. "*Id.*" may be part of a string cite. However, notice that the third citation, a reference to *Smith*, is not "*id.*" even though *Smith* is part of the immediately preceding citation. This is because "*id.*" cannot be used to refer to a single source within a string cite. When you think about it, this makes sense. If the second citation above were followed by "*id.*" the reader would likely think you intended a citation to both of the sources in the string cite.

When circumstances do not allow you to use "*id.*," you must use an abbreviated form of the full citation. Although Rule 10.9 tells us that in formulating our short form we may use (i) both parties' names; (ii) one party's name or (iii) neither party's name, B5.2 allows the use of only alternatives (ii) and (iii) in legal memoranda and court documents. In addition, you must retain the volume number of the reporter and the reporter abbreviation. However, you do not include the first page on which your case appears, but instead you give the number of the page on which you wish to focus your reader's attention, preceded by the word "at." You drop the court and date parenthetical completely:

*Party*, Vol. Reporter at Pg.

or

Vol. Reporter at Pg.

Therefore, if you wanted to formulate a short form to refer to page 33 of the case *Gagnon v. Adamson*, 264 P.2d 31 (Cal. 1953), under B5.2 you would have two options:

*Gagnon*, 264 P.2d at 33.

or

264 P.2d at 33.

Either of these forms is acceptable, but you may develop your own preference or decide that in certain situations one form is clearer than the other.

Most legal writers choose to include one party's name in an abbreviated short form. In addition, most legal writers choose to refer to a case by the party's name that appears first in the case name, and the new B5.2 reflects this usage by requiring the use of the name of the first party.

However, B5.2 warns you not to use the name of the first party if that party is frequently a party to litigation, such as a state, the United States, a governmental agency, or the head of an agency or branch of government of either a state or the United States. Therefore, for the case *State v. Roach*, 772 A.2d 395 (N.J. 2001), you would choose as your short form

*Roach*, 772 A.2d at 400.

NOT:

*State*, 772 A.2d at 400.

If the full citation of your case is a parallel citation with two or more reporter references, then craft your abbreviated short form in accordance with B5.2. Again, you would drop the first page on which your case appears in each reporter and the court and date parenthetical, but include the relevant page information for each reporter preceded by the word "at."

*Roach*, 167 N.J. at 600, 772 A.2d at 400.

For the use of "*id.*" with a parallel citation, you would include the volume and reporter information of all reporters but the official state reporter, which appears first in your citation.

*Id.* at 255, 264 P.2d at 33.

**Checklist for Case Short Forms**

- Did you cite to the current case in the immediately preceding citation? If so, use "*id.*" If not, then you cannot use "*id.*" and must use an abbreviated short form.
- Does the immediately preceding citation contain more than one authority, *i.e.*, is it a string cite? If so, then you cannot use "*id.*" and must use an abbreviated short form.
- If you cannot use "*id.*," have you formulated an acceptable abbreviated short form?
- In your abbreviated short form, have you retained the volume and reporter name from the full legal citation?
- If the full citation contained a parallel citation, have you included references to both reporters in the short form?
- In your abbreviated short form, have you used the word "at" and a pinpoint page number?

## Exercise 5
## Short Forms (Cases)

Put the following information in correct *Bluebook* citation form. All cases are being cited in citation sentences. Although this exercise builds on the rules used in previous exercises, this exercise focuses on B5.2 and Rules 4.1 and 10.9. Although the Bluepages teach us two alternatives for short forms that are equally acceptable, follow the instructions in each question for formulating short forms. In composing the short forms of party names, be guided by the information in each citation problem. For each question, you must use the correct typeface given in B13 and correct spacing given in Rule 6.1.

**1.** In the immediately preceding sentence of a legal memorandum, without an intervening cite, you cited to *Three Boys Music Corp. v. Bolton*, 212 F.3d 477 (9th Cir. 2000). You will refer to this case as "*Three Boys Music*" for the rest of the memorandum.

______________________________________________

______________________________________________

**2.** A few paragraphs later, after citing to other cases and a statute, you wish to cite to page 481 of *Three Boys Music Corp. v. Bolton*, 212 F.3d 477 (9th Cir. 2000). You have been referring to this case in text as "*Three Boys Music*."

______________________________________________

______________________________________________

**3.** On page 3 of your memorandum, you cited to *Pac. Bell v. Pub. Utils. Comm'n*, 93 Cal. Rptr. 2d 910 (Ct. App. 2000). In the same general discussion on page 5 of your memo, you would like to cite to *Pacific Bell* again, only you would like to focus your reader's attention on information beginning on page 911 and continuing on page 912 of the court's opinion. You have cited to other cases on pages 4 and 5 of your memo.

______________________________________________

______________________________________________

**4.** In the next sentence, you would like to cite to the same information again. No intervening cites appear between the citation in #3 and the current cite.

______________________________________________

______________________________________________

**5.** In the same legal memorandum, you again wish to refer to *Pac. Bell v. Pub. Utils. Comm'n*, 93 Cal. Rptr. 2d 910 (Ct. App. 2000), focusing your reader's attention on information on page 911. The immediately preceding citation sentence reads: "*Pac. Bell*, 93 Cal. Rptr. 2d at 912; *S. Cal. Edison Co.*, 102 Cal. Rptr. 2d at 685."

______________________________________________

______________________________________________

6. In a brief to a Maryland court, you have previously cited to *Dempsey v. State*, 277 Md. 134, 355 A.2d 455 (1976). You wish to cite to *Dempsey* again after several intervening cites, focusing your reader's attention on information found at page 456 of the *Atlantic Reporter* and page 137 of the *Maryland Reports*.

______________________________________________

______________________________________________

7. In the next sentence, without any intervening cites you would like to cite to *Dempsey* again, only this time you would like to direct your reader's attention to information found at page 457 of the *Atlantic Reporter* and page 138 of the *Maryland Reports*. [Note: The full citation for *Dempsey* is *Dempsey v. State*, 277 Md. 134, 355 A.2d 455 (1976).]

______________________________________________

______________________________________________

8. On page 22 of a brief to the United States Court of Appeals for the Fifth Circuit, you cite to *Wood v. United States*, 17 F. Supp. 521 (Ct. Cl. 1937). In the same general discussion on page 26 of your brief, you would like to refer to this case again, focusing your reader's attention on information beginning on page 523 and continuing on page 524 of the court's opinion. You have cited to other cases in the interim.

______________________________________________

______________________________________________

9. You wish to formulate a short form, not "*id.*," for information found on the first page of *Chi. Cent. & Pac. R.R. v. Union Pac. R.R.*, 558 N.W.2d 711 (Iowa 1997). You have referred to this case in text as "*Chicago Central*."

______________________________________________

______________________________________________

10. Immediately after citing to *Sledge v. Alsup*, 759 S.W.2d 1 (Tex. 1988), you wish to formulate a string cite, focusing your reader's attention first on page 2 of *Sledge*, and then on page 644 of *Willis v. Maverick*, 760 S.W.2d 642 (Tex. 1988), which you have not yet cited.

______________________________________________

______________________________________________

# Chapter 6
# FEDERAL STATUTES

The general rules for citing federal statutes are located in Chapter 12 of *The Bluebook*. Be aware, however, that the examples of statutory citations you will see in *The Bluebook* are printed in LARGE AND SMALL CAPITAL LETTERS. The corresponding Bluepages sections, B6.1.1 and B6.1.2, use normal typeface in their examples for statutes and constitutions. Rule B13 does not list statute names as one of the few elements of a citation that should not appear in ordinary roman type. You will remember that the ICW expects (and most legal employers and judges expect) you to use the rules in the Bluepages for legal memoranda and court documents. Therefore, you will use ordinary roman type (upper and lower case letters) rather than large and small capitals. [1] In addition to B6.1.1, you will also need to be familiar with Rules 3.2, 3.4, 6.1, and 6.2 and the federal portion of T.1. Also, although the United States Constitution is not technically a statute, it is included in this exercise, so you will also use B7 and Rule 11 of *The Bluebook*.

Both the federal statutes and the United States Constitution are published in an official compilation, the *United States Code*. The federal statutes compiled in the *United States Code* are divided into fifty subject matter areas called "titles." Each title is numbered and may span more than one hard-bound volume. Within each title, each statute is given a section number and may be divided into subsections.

To get a start on federal statutory citation form, look at the citations analyzed in B6.1.1 and Rule 12 of *The Bluebook*. The basic "formula" for a federal statute citation follows:

Title U.S.C. § Section (Date).

Rule 12.3.1(a) tells you to include the official or popular name of a statute and original section number only if the statute is commonly known by its name or if the inclusion of that information would be helpful. In most cases, you may omit the name of the statute. However, the new text of B6.1.1 seems to imply that inclusion of the official name is always required. The authors suggest that writers use their judgment as to whether inclusion of the title is helpful.

Clean Water Act, 33 U.S.C. § 1314(a)(1) (2000).

Otherwise, the first required component of the citation is the title number, which is analogous to a case citation's volume number. In a federal statutory citation, the title number precedes the name of the code cited just as the volume number of a case reporter precedes the name of the reporter in a case citation. The section number(s) follows the abbreviated code just as the page number follows the abbreviated reporter name in a case citation:

123 U.S. 456

28 U.S.C. § 1291

You cite individual code sections by using a single section symbol (§) followed by the section number. Rule 6.2(c) tells you to insert a space between the section symbol and the section number. To indicate that you are citing to more than one

---

[1] To add to the confusion, cases in West reporters sometimes present statute and rule citations in ALL CAPS. Do not copy wholesale citations you see in cases! West publications do not adhere to Bluebook form.

numbered section, use a double section symbol (§§) followed by the section numbers. Rule 3.3(b) requires a single section symbol if citing to multiple subsections within one section; use a double section symbol if citing to multiple subsections within different sections. Rule 3.3(b) also tells you to indicate a span of consecutive sections or subsections by using a hyphen between the inclusive numbers. (*The Bluebook* does not allow for the use of "*et seq.*"). To cite to nonconsecutive sections or subsections, use a comma to separate the section numbers.

28 U.S.C. §§ 1331-1367, 1441-1452 (2000).

28 U.S.C. §§ 1331, 1441 (2000).

Note, however, that you do not use double section symbols when you are citing to multiple subsections within the same numbered section.

28 U.S.C. § 1367(a)-(b) (2000).

When citing multiple subsubsections of a statute, you will generally follow the same rules as those for citing sections. When dealing with subsubsections, you will not repeat digits or letters.

28 U.S.C. § 105(b)(1), (5)

19 U.S.C. § 1490(a)(1)(A)-(C)

NOT:

28 U.S.C. § 105(b)(1), (b)(5)

19 U.S.C. § 1490(a)(1)(A)-(a)(1)(C)

Look again at the full citations given above. The last element in each is a year in parentheses. The U.S.C. main volumes are published every six years. The code is kept up to date between complete publications by annual supplements. When you are researching and citing federal statutes, you must make sure that the statutory provisions you are using and citing are the ones currently in effect. If you are researching on a commercial database, note that references are to the *United States Code Annotated* or other unofficial code that is continuously updated.

If all of your cited material appears in the main volume, then you simply include the year the main volume was published. If all of your cited material appears in a supplement, then you indicate this by including the abbreviation "Supp." and the year the supplement was published. If your reader would need to consult both the main volume and the supplement, then you must include both pieces of information connected by an ampersand (&).

Title U.S.C. § Section (Year & Supp. Year).

You will need to also refer to T.1 to make sure you are citing the appropriate code. T.1 tells you to cite to the *United States Code* if the statute is found therein. (See the note in T.1 beside the heading "Statutory compilations.") Otherwise, you may cite to the *United States Code Annotated*, *United States Code Service*, or *United States Code Unannotated*, in that order of preference.

Let's walk through a federal statutory citation to get you started. Let's put section 501 of title 17 of the *United States Code* into a citation sentence. Subsection (a) of the statute is in the 2004 Supplement, but all remaining provisions are in the main volume, published in 2000. We are not using the name of the act of which this statute is a part, so you know from Rule 12 that the first element of a federal statutory citation is the number of the title. In our statute that number is 17. Next is the abbreviation of the code. Following the information on federal courts, T.1 shows the proper abbreviations and formats for "Statutory compilations." You see that the abbreviation for the *United States Code* is "U.S.C." Rule 6.1(a) tells you to close up adjacent single capitals, so make sure there are no spaces in "U.S.C."

17 U.S.C.

Next comes a section symbol followed by a space. After the section symbol and space, you will insert the section number.

17 U.S.C. § 501

The final element is the year. You already know that the statute is currently in force and that you are citing the official code. Therefore, according to B6.1.1 and Rule 12.3.1(d), and as shown in T.1, you do not have to show the name of a publisher. You know also that the main volumes of the current official code were published in 2000. The *United States Code* is kept up to date between complete publications by annual supplements, and the current Supplement was published in 2004.[2] Because our statute is in both the main volume and supplement, both dates must be included.

Therefore, our finished citation sentence is the following:

17 U.S.C. § 501 (2000 & Supp. 2004).

In addition to these rules for citing most statutes, you do need to know some rules for some specific statutes; these details are in Rule 12.8 and B6.1.3 through B6.1.5. For example, when citing to the current version of the Internal Revenue Code, you should cite to "I.R.C." rather than to title 26 of the *United States Code*. In that case, you would omit the date parenthetical according to rule B6.1.5.

I.R.C. § 703(a).

NOT:

26 U.S.C. § 703(a) (2000).

Similarly, B6.1.3 and Rule 12.8.3 tell us that cites to the current version of certain rules, such as the Federal Rules of Civil Procedure, which are published in an appendix to the *United States Code*, do not cite to the *United States Code*, but instead cite only to the rules themselves. A citation to the current version of the rule does not require a date parenthetical.

Fed. R. Civ. P. 26(b)(4).

---

2 The unofficial codes publish annual supplements for each separate volume. The supplements are inserted into pockets inside the back covers of the bound volumes and thus have come to be known as "pocket parts." When a pocket part becomes too bulky to fit conveniently into the pocket, the publisher puts out a softbound "cumulative supplement" which serves the same purpose but does not go inside the bound volume.

**Checklist for Federal Statutes**

- If you are using the name of the statute, have you put that name first?
- Have you put the title number before the name of the code?
- Have you properly abbreviated the name of the code?
- Have you closed up (left no spaces between) all adjacent single capitals in the abbreviated name of the code?
- Have you inserted a single section symbol for a single statute and a double section symbol for more than one statute?
- Have you left a single space between the section symbol and the section number?
- Have you closed up the section number and its subsections?
- Have you put the year(s) of publication in parentheses at the end of your citation?
- If any portion of your cited material is included in a supplementary volume, have you indicated this in the date parenthetical?
- Have you left a space between the last character of the section number and the date parenthetical?
- Have you ended your citation sentence with a period?

## Exercise 6
## Federal Statutes

Put the following information in correct *Bluebook* citation form. All statutes are being cited in citation sentences. This exercise focuses on B6.1.1, Rules 12.2, 12.3, 12.8, 11, and 3.4(b). You will also need to refer to T.1 for information on federal statutes. For each question, you must use the correct typeface given in B13 and the correct spacing given in Rule 6.1.

1. Article one, section eight of the Constitution of the United States.

___

___

2. Section 87f-1, subsection (a)(4), of title 7 of the current *United States Code*, published in 2000. No amendments to this section appear in any supplement or pocket part.

___

___

3. Subsections (a) through (d) of section 204 of title 23 of the current *United States Code*, published in 2000. No amendments to this section appear in any supplement or pocket part.

___

___

4. Subsections (a)(1)(A) through (a)(1)(C) of section 1251 of title 8 of the current *United States Code*. Part of this citation appears in the 2000 main volume, and part appears in the 2004 supplement.

___

___

5. Subsection 14071(e)(2) of title 42 of the current *United States Code*. Part of this citation appears in the 2000 main volume, and part appears in the 2004 supplement.

___

___

6. Subsection (1)(C) of section 303 of title 37 of the current *United States Code*, published in 2000.

___

___

7. Section 5003 of title 12 of the current *United States Code*, published in 2000. The entire text of this section appears in the 2004 supplement.

___

___

8. Rule 1331(a) of the current Federal Rules of Civil Procedure, published in 2000 in the Appendix to title 28 of the *United States Code*.

___

___

**9.** Section 706(d)(2) of the current Internal Revenue Code, published in 2000 in title 26 of the current *United States Code.*

________________________________________

________________________________________

**10.** Rule 20 of the Federal Rules of Criminal Procedure, published in 2000 in the Appendix to title 28 of the *United States Code.*

________________________________________

________________________________________

# Chapter 7
# STATE STATUTES

B6.1.2 and Rules 12.3.1 and 12.3.2 generally govern statute citations. Remember from Chapter 6 that B6 and B13 tells us that all text in the statute citation should be in ordinary roman type for legal memoranda and court documents, not large and small capitals as indicated by Rule 12. Please read these rules carefully before attempting Exercise 7.

The citation form for federal statutes and state statutes is similar; however, the challenge here is that each state has a different system of compiling and publishing statutes. Thus, each state has a slightly different citation form for statutes. Generally, each citation will include the following:

- an abbreviated name of the state code (just as with the U.S.C., the name of the code will not use LARGE AND SMALL CAPITAL LETTERS)
- possibly the name of a subject matter if the code is arranged by subject matter;
- numerical information pointing the reader to a specific statutory provision;
- possibly the publisher of the code; and
- the year of publication.

In each state's entry in T.1, you will find a template for what information to include and in what form. This table also includes the proper abbreviation for each state code. Therefore, for each state statute that you cite, you should always refer to that state's page in T.1 for a fool-proof "formula." You may also need to consult Rule 6.1(a) to ensure that you are spacing the abbreviation correctly.

Most statutes are not organized by pages as cases are. Instead, most statutes are arranged by sections, but may also be arranged by chapters, titles, paragraphs, subdivisions, or a combination thereof. Therefore, in addition to consulting T.1, you will also need to pay attention to Rule 3.3 with regard to sections and paragraphs. Broadly, remember that you indicate that you are citing to multiple sections by using two section symbols without a space in between. Note, however, that you need a space between the section symbol and the actual section number.

Ariz. Rev. Stat. §§ 17-454, 17-456 (2006).

Del. Code Ann. tit. 3, § 10105(a) (2001).

Alaska Stat. § 37.14.400 (2006).

The only other detail you need to know to master the basics of state statute citation is how to determine the date of the code. Note that the year of the code is NOT the date the particular statute was enacted. To avoid this confusion, remember the purpose of the date in the citation: to help your reader know how to find a particular statute. To do this, your reader must know what version of a code to consult, *i.e.*, the version of the code published in a particular year. In addition, your reader must know whether the information is contained in the main body of the code, a supplement or pocket part, or both. Therefore, you need to include this information. Generally, the year of the code will appear on the spine of the volume, the title page, or elsewhere as a copyright date. *The Bluebook* tells you to use the date appearing in one of these places, in the preceding order of preference. If the entirety of the section that you are citing appears in the main volume, use only the date for the main volume.

Del. Code Ann. tit. 7, § 931 (2001).

Often, part or all of the section will have been amended and reprinted in a supplementary volume that is either bound separately from the main volume or attached in a pocket located in the inside back cover of the main volume. In that case, include the years for both the main volume and the supplement.

Del. Code Ann. tit. 7, § 927 (2001 & Supp. 2006).

Many times, a newly enacted statute will appear only in the supplement or pocket part. In these cases, you should only include the year of the supplement, preceded by "Supp." pursuant to Rule 3.1(c).

Del. Code Ann. tit. 7, § 517(c) (Supp. 2006).

Some states, such as California and Michigan, have more than one statutory compilation. Generally, *The Bluebook* prefers citations to the official state code, if possible. T.1 informs you which compilation to cite to in order of preference. However, most law libraries only subscribe to one set of state statutes for each state. Some compilations require you to include the publisher in the date parenthetical. If so, the publisher would be included in the formula given in T.1.

Alaska Stat. § 37.14.400 (1998).

Lastly, states such as Texas and New York with subject matter codes use a "formula" that indicates where the subject of the code should be "plugged in" to the citation. The names of the subjects are abbreviated according to T.6.

Tex. [subject] Code Ann. § x (Vernon year).

The brackets indicate the place holder for the name of the subject; once the subject is included, the brackets are omitted.

Tex. Gov't Code Ann. § x (Vernon year).

NOT:

Tex [Gov't] Code Ann. § x (Vernon year).

## Checklist for State Statutes

- Have you consulted T.1 for the correct abbreviation of the state code?
- Have you followed the format for the state statute given in T.1?
- Have you taken the year of the code from the spine, title page, or copyright information in the appropriate volume?
- Does all of the information cited appear in the main volume?
    - If so, then include only the year of the main volume in the parenthetical.
    - If a portion of the statute cited is in a supplement, then include the date of the main volume and the supplement.
- Does all of the information cited appear in a supplement? If so, then include the date of only the supplement.
- For states with subject matter codes, have you omitted the brackets used in the T.1 formula and abbreviated according to T.6?

## Exercise 7
## State Statutes

Put the following information in correct *Bluebook* citation form. All statutes are being cited in citation sentences. Although this exercise builds on the rules used in previous exercises, this exercise focuses on state rather than federal statutes. You will need to refer to T.1 for information on the statutes in the appropriate jurisdiction. For each question, you must use the correct typeface given in B13 and the correct spacing given in Rule 6.1.

1. Section 35-4-20 of the *Code of Alabama*, published by LexisNexis in 1991. No amendments to this section appear in any supplement or pocket part.

 ____________________________________________________________

 ____________________________________________________________

2. Section 27-803(3) of the *Revised Statutes of Nebraska Annotated*, published by LexisNexis in 1995. The entire text of this subsection appears in the 2006 supplement.

 ____________________________________________________________

 ____________________________________________________________

3. Section 61-2-100(B) of the *Code of Laws of South Carolina 1976 Annotated*, published by West. The entire text of this subsection appears in the 2008 cumulative supplement.

 ____________________________________________________________

 ____________________________________________________________

4. Section 24:16B-63 of the *New Jersey Statutes Annotated*, published by West. The copyright date is 1997. No amendments to this section appear in any supplement or pocket part.

 ____________________________________________________________

 ____________________________________________________________

5. Sections 10-9-18 and 10-9-21 of the *New Mexico Statutes 1978*. Part of this citation appears in the 2003 main volume, and part appears in the 2006 cumulative supplement.

 ____________________________________________________________

 ____________________________________________________________

6. Section 4303.33, subsections (A) and (C) of Page's *Ohio Revised Code Annotated*, published by LexisNexis. Both of these subsections appear in their entirety in the 2003 main volume.

 ____________________________________________________________

 ____________________________________________________________

7. Section 3205, subsection (a), of the *California Government Code*, part of West's *Annotated California Code*, published in 1995. The entire text of subsection (a) appears in the 2008 cumulative pocket part.

 ____________________________________________________________

 ____________________________________________________________

**8.** Section 39-1-1, subsections (a) through (b), of the *Official Code of Georgia Annotated*, published by LexisNexis. The date on the title page is 1995. No amendments to this section appear in any supplement or pocket part.

______________________________________________________________________

______________________________________________________________________

**9.** Section 679A.2 of the *Iowa Code Annotated*, published by West. The copyright of the main volume is 1998. No amendments to this section appear in any pocket part or supplement.

______________________________________________________________________

______________________________________________________________________

**10.** Title 21, sections 692 through 694, of the *Oklahoma Statutes Annotated*, published by West. The date on the copyright page is 2002. No amendments to these sections appear in any supplement or pocket part.

______________________________________________________________________

______________________________________________________________________

**11.** Section 37:788(A) of West's *Louisiana Revised Statutes Annotated*, published by West. The copyright of the main volume is 2007. No amendments to this section appear in any supplement or pocket part.

______________________________________________________________________

______________________________________________________________________

**12.** Section 491.050 of Vernon's *Annotated Missouri Statutes*, published by West. No amendments to this section appear in any supplement or pocket part. The copyright date is 1996.

______________________________________________________________________

______________________________________________________________________

**13.** Section 416.675, subsections (1) and (3), of Michie's *Kentucky Revised Statutes Annotated*, published by LexisNexis. These subsections appear in their entirety in the 2007 cumulative supplement.

______________________________________________________________________

______________________________________________________________________

**14.** Sections 8-6-503(4) and 8-6-504 of the *Arkansas Code of 1987 Annotated*, published by LexisNexis. Part of this citation appears in the 2000 main volume, and part appears in the 2007 cumulative supplement.

______________________________________________________________________

______________________________________________________________________

**15.** Section 911 of title 2 of the *Delaware Code Annotated*, published by LexisNexis. This section appears in the 2001 main volume.

______________________________________________________________________

______________________________________________________________________

# Chapter 8
# SHORT FORMS (STATUTES)

As with cases, you will often refer to a statute several times within a legal memorandum or a court document. Similarly, *The Bluebook* states that you need to give the full legal citation for a statute only the *first* time that you cite to that statute. As long as subsequent references to the same statute appear in the same general discussion, you may use a short form citation to that statute. B6.2 and Rules 4.1(b) and 12.9 provide information on short form citations for state and federal statutes. (Note that the last rule in each chapter generally deals with short forms for sources discussed within that chapter.) You should read each of those sections carefully before attempting Exercise 8. B7 and Rule 11 tell us that the only acceptable short form for a constitution is "*id.*" Otherwise, use the full form.

As with cases, *The Bluebook* provides two types of short forms to be used for statutes in legal memoranda and court documents: "*id.*" and an abbreviated version of the full legal citation. The rules for when you may use each type parallel the rules that we discussed in connection with cases. You may use the short form "*id.*" only when you are citing to a statute previously cited in the immediately preceding citation (and only if that previous citation is not a string cite). Again, no intervening cites to a different authority of any type should appear between the previous cite to this statute and the current citation.

You learned in Exercise 5 (Short Forms (Cases)) that you use "*id.*" to refer to a previous case even when you want to cite to a different page. Similarly, the previous citation to a statute need not be to the exact section or subsection of your statute; however, you will need to include any information in your citation that differs from the immediately preceding citation. Unlike case short forms, however, statutory short forms never use the word "at," as detailed in Rule 3.3. The proper formulation is simply the word "*id.*" followed immediately by the new section or subsection information. Because Rule 4.1 tells you that you should indicate in an "*id.*" cite only the way in which that citation differs from the previous one; you will omit the code abbreviation and the date and publisher parenthetical, provided that the material is the same for the "*id.*" cite as for the original citation. However, you should reproduce the entire section number for clarity. Notice in the example below that the second citation includes both the section and subsection information rather than just the different subsection. Notice that the third citation includes also the date parenthetical because section 1–201(b)(4) is in the 2003 Supplement, but the original section cited was in the 1997 main volume.

> In our jurisdiction, "fruit" is defined as an edible part of a plant that contains seeds. **St. Stat. Ann. § 1–201(a) (1997).** A "vegetable" is defined as an edible part of a plant that does not contain seeds. ***Id.* § 1-201(b)(1).** However, the term "vegetable" does not include legumes or tubers. ***Id.*** Recently, the legislature determined that a cucumber, although it contains seeds, would be deemed to be a vegetable. ***Id.* § 1-201(b)(4) (Supp. 2003).**

In those circumstances when you wish to use a short form but cannot use "*id.*," you will use an abbreviated form of the full citation. Rule 12.9 provides a chart of acceptable short forms, and B6.2 incorporates the chart by reference. For federal statutes, you may retain the volume and abbreviation for the *United States Code* in addition to the section number or retain only the section number.

36 U.S.C. § 301 (2000).

becomes:

36 U.S.C. § 301.

OR

§ 301.

Depending on the compilation strategy of a particular state code, you may not have many options in composing your short form; at other times, you may have an option as to how much information to retain, as in the *Delaware Code Annotated* example in Rule 12.9. Generally, you omit all references to the name of the code and the date of publication information and retain all numerical information relating to the statute. For instance, if the state code is organized only by sections, such as the *Maryland Code*, then you simply omit the code name information and retain the section number.

Md. Code Ann., Fin. Inst. § 13–708.1 (West 2003).

becomes:

§ 13–708.1.

However, some state codes, such as *General Laws of the Commonwealth of Massachusetts*, are divided into titles or chapters and then further into sections. For those state statutes, you may retain all of the numerical information or merely the section number.

Mass. Gen. Laws ch. 4, § 7 (Supp. 2008).

becomes:

Ch. 4, § 7.

OR

§ 7.

You will eventually develop your own preference, but your ultimate objective should be absolute clarity for your reader.

## Checklist for Statutory Short Forms

- Did you cite to the current statute in the immediately preceding citation? If not, then you cannot use "*id.*"
- Does the immediately preceding citation contain more than one authority, *i.e.*, is it a string cite? If so, then you cannot use "*id.*"
- If you cannot use "*id.*," have you formulated an acceptable abbreviated short form?
- Have you remembered not to include the word "at" in your short form?

## Exercise 8
## Short Forms (Statutes)

Put the following information in correct *Bluebook* citation form. All statutes are being cited in citation sentences. Although this exercise builds on the rules used in previous exercises, this exercise focuses on B7 and Rules 4.1, 11, and 12.9. You will need to refer to T.1 for information on the statutes in the appropriate jurisdiction. For each question, you must use the correct typeface given in B13 and the correct spacing given in Rule 6.1.

**1.** In the immediately preceding sentence of a legal memorandum, you cited to a provision of the *Arkansas Code of 1987 Annotated*, Ark. Code Ann. § 24-4-712(d) (2000). Without an intervening cite, you wish to cite to subsection (b) of this same statute.

______________________________________________

______________________________________________

**2.** On the next page of your memorandum, after citing to several other authorities, you wish to cite again to Ark. Code Ann. § 24-4-712(d) (2000).

______________________________________________

______________________________________________

**3.** In the very next sentence of your memorandum, without an intervening cite, you wish to cite to the same subsection (a).

______________________________________________

______________________________________________

**4.** Earlier in the same general discussion, you cited to 42 U.S.C. § 601(a)(1) (2000). Now, two pages later, you wish to cite to subsection (a)(3). Several cites to other authorities appear on the two intervening pages.

______________________________________________

______________________________________________

**5.** In a legal memorandum, you cited to a provision of the *Official Code of Georgia Annotated*, Ga. Code Ann. § 37-1-20(b)(1) (1995). In the next line, you again cite to the same provision, using the short form "*id.*" In the next paragraph, without any intervening cites, you wish to cite to subsection (b)(2) of the same provision.

______________________________________________

______________________________________________

**6.** In the same paragraph, following a cite to a case construing subsection (b)(2), you wish to cite to Ga. Code Ann. § 37-1-20(c) (1995).

______________________________________________

______________________________________________

**7.** In an appellate brief, you wish to cite to section 21-I:52 of the *New Hampshire Revised Statutes Annotated*. The immediately preceding cite reads N.H. Rev. Stat. Ann. § 21-J:29 (Supp. 2007); *State Employees' Ass'n of N.H., Inc. v. Pub. Employee Relations Bd.*, 397 A.2d 1035 (N.H. 1978).

______________________________________________

______________________________________________

**8.** In a legal memorandum, you have previously cited to an Arizona statute, Ariz. Rev. Stat. Ann. § 31-411(D) (2002). A few paragraphs later, with several intervening cites to different authorities, you wish to cite to subsection (E).

______________________________________________

______________________________________________

**9.** In the next sentence, without any intervening cites, you wish to cite to Ariz. Rev. Stat. Ann. § 31-411(D) (2002).

______________________________________________

______________________________________________

**10.** In a legal memorandum, you have previously cited to a portion of the United States Constitution, U.S. Const. art. III, § 2, cl. 2. After several intervening cites to other authorities, you wish to cite to the same provision.

______________________________________________

______________________________________________

# Chapter 9
# COMPREHENSIVE CORE EXERCISE

After completing the first eight exercises, you are well on your way to mastering legal citation! Let's stop, catch our breath, and review what you have learned.

By now, you should know how to cite any case decided by a court in the United States, whether state or federal. Also, if you are citing a case to a state court and that state requires parallel citation to a state reporter and a regional reporter, you know how to construct that parallel citation. You also know how to use "*id.*" and how to formulate short forms for case citations.

Similarly, you know how to cite to any statute, state or federal. You are also comfortable using "*id.*" and short forms to refer to statutes that you have already referenced in a full citation.

With these skills, you can cite to most authoritative sources and produce a professional legal memorandum or court document. In the next exercises, we are going to introduce you to the concept of citation signals, which "signal" to your reader the importance of citations if the connection between the source and your proposition is not clear in the text alone. You will also learn how to add explanatory parentheticals to your citations to reinforce and clarify the importance of those citations. We will also explore other types of sources, such as books, treatises, law review articles, and legislative resources.

Before we continue marching on, you may want to try Exercise 9: Comprehensive Core Exercise, which will reinforce the skills learned in Exercises 1–8. To help you get back into the swing of things, the following is a list of common mistakes first-year law students make in basic citation:

- Forgetting to put a court designation in the court and date parenthetical when the reporter information is not sufficient.
- Guessing on the abbreviations in case names instead of checking T.6.
- Omitting the volume and reporter information in a case short form: *e.g.*, "*Casper*, 99 U.S. at 310," **not** "*Casper*, at 310."
- Omitting the comma between the case name and the volume information in a case short form.
- Omitting the space between "F." and "Supp." and "Supp." and "2d" for cases reported in *Federal Supplement* ("F. Supp." and "F. Supp. 2d").
- Omitting a date parenthetical in a full citation of a statute.

Finally, remember your successful completion of these exercises does not mean that you should never consult *The Bluebook* again. Most student citation mistakes arise when students think they remember what *The Bluebook* says, but do not actually look up the rule. The best legal writers are not those who memorize *The Bluebook*, but those who know when to open it.

## Exercise 9
## Comprehensive Core Exercise

Put the following information in correct *Bluebook* citation form. Assume that the authority is being cited in citation sentences in a brief to the United States Supreme Court unless otherwise noted. For each question, you must use the correct typeface given in B13 and the correct spacing given in Rule 6.1. This exercise reviews the skills you learned in Exercises 1 through 8.

1. John Gregory, et al., versus the United States of America. This case was decided in the United States Court of Appeals for the Sixth Circuit on May 4, 1979. It appears in volume 597, page 1087, of *Federal Reporter*, Second Series. You wish to direct your reader to information on page 1088.

______________________________________________

______________________________________________

2. On page 4 of a legal memorandum, you cited the case above. In the same general discussion on page 6, you would like to refer to the case in #1 again, this time focusing your reader's attention on information beginning on page 1089 of the opinion and continuing through page 1090. You have cited to other cases in the interim, so a short form with a case name would be helpful to your reader.

______________________________________________

______________________________________________

3. Section 27-6-27 of the *General Laws of Rhode Island*. The date on the copyright page is 2002, and no amendments to this section appear in any pocket part or supplement.

______________________________________________

______________________________________________

4. You wish to cite again to section 27-6-27 of the *General Laws of Rhode Island* in the next paragraph of an appellate brief. You have cited to two cases interpreting section 27-6-27 since your last reference to it.

______________________________________________

______________________________________________

5. William Earl Avery, Appellant, versus the State of Alabama, Appellee. This case was decided in the Alabama Court of Criminal Appeals in 1991. It is reported in volume 589, page 1313, of *Southern Reporter*, Second Series.

______________________________________________

______________________________________________

6. Section 3142, subsection (a), of title 18 of the *United States Code*, published in 2000.

______________________________________________

______________________________________________

**7.** One paragraph later, after citing to a provision of the United States Constitution, you wish to cite again to Section 3142, subsection (a), of title 18 of the *United States Code*. You have been referring to this section in text as "Section 3142(a)."

______________________________________________

______________________________________________

**8.** Sections 184.702 of West's *Minnesota Statutes Annotated*. Parts of these sections appear in the 2002 main volume, but some portions were added in the 2008 pocket part.

______________________________________________

______________________________________________

**9.** Sandra Boddie, plaintiff-appellant, versus American Broadcasting Companies, Inc., Charles C. Thompson, executive producer, and Geraldo Rivera, senior producer, defendants-appellees. This 1984 case from the United States Court of Appeals for the Sixth Circuit is reported in volume 731, page 333, of *Federal Reporter*, Second Series. [Note: American Broadcasting Companies, Inc., is commonly referred to by its initials, ABC.]

______________________________________________

______________________________________________

**10.** In a brief to the Illinois Supreme Court, you cite McDonald's Corporation, Noel Kaplan, and Dean Canterbury versus William S. Levine, Gene Himmelstein, Stephen Haberkorn, and W. Yale Matheson. This case was decided by an Illinois Appellate Court in 1982. This decision is reported in volume 108, page 732, of *Illinois Appellate Court Reports*, Third Series, and in volume 439, page 475, of *North Eastern Reporter*, Second Series. Assume that the usual practice in Illinois is to cite both state and regional reporters.

______________________________________________

______________________________________________

**11.** In the sentence immediately following the citation in #10, you wish to refer to the same case. This time, however, you would like to direct your reader's attention to information found on page 736 of *Illinois Appellate Court Reports*, Third Series, and on page 478 of volume 439 of *North Eastern Reporter*, Second Series.

______________________________________________

______________________________________________

**12.** The current text of Federal Rule of Civil Procedure 5, published in the appendix to title 28 of the *United States Code*. The entire text of this rule appears in the 2000 main volume.

______________________________________________

______________________________________________

**13.** Section 157.162 of Vernon's *Texas Family Code Annotated*. The entire provision appears in the 2007 cumulative supplement.

______________________________________________

______________________________________________

**14.** In a brief to a Texas state district court, you wish to cite Marion Conser versus Earlene Biddy. This case was decided in the Supreme Court of Arkansas on December 7, 1981. It is published in volume 274, page 367, of *Arkansas Reports*, and in volume 625, page 457, of *South Western Reporter*, Second Series.

______________________________________________

______________________________________________

**15.** You wish to cite to the case in #14 two pages later in your brief, after several intervening cites, so a short form with a case name would be helpful to your reader. You want to direct your reader's attention to material that appears on page 370 of the state reporter and 460 of the regional reporter.

______________________________________________

______________________________________________

**16.** Associated General Contractors of California, Incorporated, versus the City of San Francisco. This case was decided by the United States District Court for the Central District of California in 1985. It is reported in volume 619, page 334, of *Federal Supplement.*

______________________________________________

______________________________________________

**17.** Section 48.20.022 of West's *Revised Code of Washington Annotated.* The date on the copyright page is 1999. No amendments to this section appear in any supplement or pocket part.

______________________________________________

______________________________________________

**18.** In the next sentence, without any intervening cites, you wish to cite to section 48.20.025 of West's *Revised Code of Washington Annotated.* This section has been stated in its entirety in the 2001 pocket part.

______________________________________________

______________________________________________

**19.** In a trial brief to a West Virginia state trial court, you cite Stephen S. Peters versus Steve D. Narick, Judge of the Circuit Court of Marshall County. This case was decided by the Supreme Court of Appeals of West Virginia in 1980. It appears in volume 165, page 622, of *West Virginia Reports*, and in volume 270, page 760, of *South Eastern Reporter*, Second Series. Assume that the usual practice in West Virginia is to cite both state and regional reporters.

______________________________________________

______________________________________________

**20.** John and Faye Mizner, individually and on behalf of their minor children, Tiffany and Justin Mizner, versus North River Homes, Incorporated, and Cape Mobile Home Mart, Inc. This case was decided by the Missouri Court of Appeals on May 30, 1995. It appears in volume 913, page 23, of *South Western Reporter*, Second Series. You wish to focus your reader's attention to information on page 28.

______________________________________________

______________________________________________

# Chapter 10
# PRIOR & SUBSEQUENT CASE HISTORY

Now that you have mastered a basic case citation, you are ready to add a more advanced skill: prior and subsequent history. You probably have learned by now that one case may go through several levels of appeal in its life. At each level, the court reviewing the case may publish an opinion. Opinions issued by courts that review the case after the opinion you wish to cite are called *subsequent history*. Opinions issued by courts before the opinion you wish to cite are called *prior history*. As you read through this chapter, you will likely find the examples in Rules 10.7, 10.7.1, and 10.7.2, and B5.1.5 helpful. These rules tend to be fairly detailed and complex, but remember: you need not memorize any citation rules. You only need to understand how they work and where to find them so you can refresh your understanding.

The *Bluebook* quick reference for subsequent history is B5.1.5 of the Bluepages. Read this before continuing.

To illustrate this, let's use the fictional case of *Bait v. Switch*. *Bait v. Switch* started out as a negligence lawsuit in federal trial court in the Northern District of Texas. Bait was awarded damages by the trial court, and the trial court issued an opinion. This opinion was reported in *Federal Supplement*. Switch then appealed to the Fifth Circuit Court of Appeals. The Fifth Circuit affirmed the trial court's judgment and also issued an opinion, which was published in *Federal Reporter*, Third Series. Finally, Switch filed a writ of certiorari to the United States Supreme Court. The United States Supreme Court denied certiorari, issuing an opinion explaining the reason for the denial. This opinion was reported in several reporters, including *United States Reports*. So we have three different courts that have dealt with this case and issued opinions. The Fifth Circuit Court of Appeals and United States Supreme Court opinions are *subsequent history* to the federal trial court opinion.

**[N.D. Tex.]** **5th Cir.** **U.S.**

***subsequent history***

The federal trial court and Fifth Circuit opinions are *prior history* to the United States Supreme Court opinion.

**N.D. Tex.** **5th Cir.** **[U.S.]**

***prior history***

The Fifth Circuit opinion has both prior and subsequent history — the federal district court opinion is prior history, and the United States Supreme Court opinion is subsequent history.

N.D. Tex. | 5th Cir. | U.S.

*prior history* | | *subsequent history*

You will find citations to prior and subsequent history by using a citator service such as *Shepard's*. You should receive instruction on how to use a citator in your legal research class.

The rule governing when to include prior and subsequent history is Rule 10.7. As we will see shortly, you also will need to consult Rule 10.5(d) sometimes when including prior or subsequent history. *The Bluebook* tells us first **when** to include prior and subsequent history and then **how** to include it.

"When" is covered in Rule 10.7. The general rule for subsequent history is that it should be included when you cite a decision in full. (This means, then, that short cites should not include prior or subsequent history.) However, this is a rule with many exceptions. And the exceptions have exceptions.

**Include subsequent history unless . . .**

- **the history is a denial of certiorari or similar discretionary appeal**

  ***but*** include denials of cert. if the decision is less than two years old or "the denial is particularly relevant,"

- **the history is on remand or the denial of a rehearing**

  ***but*** include this type of history if it is particularly relevant to the point cited, or

- **the history is a disposition that has been withdrawn by the deciding authority.**

The general rule for prior history is that it *should not* be included. This rule also has exceptions, but they are a little easier to remember.

**Do not include prior history unless . . .**

- **the history is "significant to the point for which the case is cited" or**
- **the decision cited does not "intelligibly describe the issues in the case."**

When would a decision not "intelligibly describe" the issue? Let's go back to *Bait v. Switch*. Assume we want to cite the Fifth Circuit's opinion in *Bait v. Switch* because it is favorable to the point we are arguing. However, the Fifth Circuit opinion does not include as full a description of the facts in the case as the district court opinion does. If we wanted to analogize our facts closely to those of *Bait v. Switch* to argue that our client's case should be decided the same way the Fifth Circuit decided *Bait*, we might give the prior history of *Bait v. Switch* (the federal district court opinion) so we could use the lower court's description of the facts.

So now that we know **when** to give prior and subsequent history, we're ready to learn **how** to do it. Rule 10.7.1(a) tells us that the prior or subsequent history will follow the full citation of the primary case. This usually means that the history cite will follow the primary cite's court and date parenthetical. However, if the primary case cite includes an additional parenthetical (for explanation, weight of authority, etc. — all things we will cover in Chapter 13), then the history cite follows that parenthetical.

Our history cite will be introduced by an explanatory phrase. A partial list of these explanatory phrases appears in T.8. Notice in T.8 that some of the phrases are followed by commas and others are not. If the phrase is not followed by a comma in T.8, then do not place a comma after it in your citation. Notice also that some of the phrases are (or begin with) an *-ing* verb while others begin with an *-ed* verb. The *-ing* verbs introduce prior history and are not followed by a comma; the *-ed* verbs introduce subsequent history and are followed by a comma.

These explanatory phrases give the reader important information about the relationship between the cases cited. For example, what if we want to cite *Bait v. Switch* (the district court opinion) for Proposition A, but it has been reversed in *Switch v. Bait* (the Fifth Circuit opinion) for the lower court's error on Proposition B? Although *Bait v. Switch* is no longer good law for Proposition B, it is still good law for Proposition A. To let the reader know that we are aware of the reversal but that it has no impact on our argument, we would introduce the subsequent history cite with the explanatory phrase "*rev'd on other grounds*."

When including history, pay close attention to the date of decision for all of the cases in the citation. If two cases listed consecutively in the cite are decided in the same year, then Rule 10.5(d) tells us to note the year only in the final court and date parenthetical containing that year. What if we have three citations: the primary cite in Year A, the first subsequent history cite also in Year A, and a final subsequent history cite in Year B? In that case, include no date of decision for the primary cite, Year A as the date of decision in the first history cite, and Year B as the date of decision in the final history cite.

> *North v. South*, 111 Rptr. 222 **(Ct.)**, *rev'd*, 333 Rptr. 444 **(Ct. Year A)**, *rev'd*, 555 Rptr. 666 **(Ct. Year B)**.

Sometimes, a case requires several history citations. If we give both a prior and a subsequent history citation, Rule 10.7.1(a) tells us to list the prior history first. If we give several dispositions (either two or more prior history cites or two or more subsequent history cites), Rule 10.7.1(a) tells us to append those cites to each other, separating them with a comma. For an example, consult Rule 10.7.1(a).

Most of the subsequent history will be in the cited case's direct line. For example, all of the opinions in the *Bait v. Switch* example involve the same parties and the same litigation. However, Rule 10.7.1(c) tells us to note as subsequent history cases that overrule a cited case, regardless of whether the cases are otherwise related.

What happens if the case name changes on appeal? Rule 10.7.2 covers this. If the names are simply reversed on appeal, then we do nothing. Cite the case name as it appears in the primary case we are citing and simply give a citation without a case name for the prior or subsequent history. The same is true if the history cite is a denial of certiorari or an administrative action in which the private party is the same.

But what if the first-named party changes on either or both sides? Not all parties that are involved in one phase of a case are necessarily involved in subsequent appeals. If we want to indicate a different name for a subsequent history cite, add the phrase "*sub nom.*" to the explanatory phrase and give the case name along with the citation for the history cite. If we want to indicate a different name for prior history, simply give the case names for both the primary and prior history cite, but do not introduce the second name with "*sub nom.*"

That's a lot of explanation, but the drafting is really not bad. Let's try an example. Because we are familiar with Bait and Switch, let's use their case and assume that we have the following citations to work with:

| | |
|---|---|
| trial court: | *Bait v. Switch*, 111 F. Supp. 222 (N.D. Tex. 1994). |
| intermediate court of appeals: | *Switch v. Bait*, 333 F.3d 444 (5th Cir. 1994). |
| court of last resort: | *Switch v. Jones*, 555 U.S. 666 (1995). |
| unrelated case: | *Duck v. Cover*, 777 U.S. 888 (1997). |

First, let's assume that we want to cite the intermediate court of appeals opinion in the Bait and Switch litigation. So, we start with that citation:

*Switch v. Bait*, 333 F.3d 444 (5th Cir. 1994).

We start with the general rule that we include subsequent history. So we consider whether to include the citation to *Switch v. Jones*. If *Switch v. Jones* was simply a denial of certiorari by the United States Supreme Court, we would not include it. Why? The decision in *Switch v. Bait* is older than two years. Therefore, the denial of certiorari would not be included. However, the Supreme Court did not deny certiorari. Instead, when we look up *Switch v. Jones*, we discover that the Supreme Court heard the case and issued an opinion affirming the Fifth Circuit's decision in *Switch v. Bait.* However, it affirmed the Fifth Circuit on different grounds from those for which we intend to cite the case. First, we will need to turn to T.8 to find out what explanatory phrase to use. Sixth down from the top of the list we see "*aff'd on other grounds*," — that looks like exactly what we need. Remember that we use the *-ed* phrase because the phrase introduces subsequent history. Notice that we will replace the period at the end of the original citation sentence with a comma and save the period for the new end of our citation sentence.

*Switch v. Bait*, 333 F.3d 444 (5th Cir. 1994), *aff'd on other grounds*,

Notice also that T.8 says to use a comma after this particular explanatory phrase. Remember, commas *following* italicized text are not italicized according to Rule 2.1(f).

Now it's time for the history citation. To name or not to name. Well, the party names are not simply reversed (*Switch v. Bait* and *Switch v. Jones*), and this is not a denial of certiorari or an administrative action. Rather, we have a subsequent history citation with a different name. So follow Rule 10.7.2. and add "*sub nom.*" to the explanatory phrase and then give the case name along with the other citation information. Notice that when you add "*sub nom.*" to the explanatory phrase, you omit any comma that would otherwise follow the phrase. This is one of those rules that is given by example rather than explicitly.

*Switch v. Bait*, 333 F.3d 444 (5th Cir. 1994), *aff'd on other grounds sub nom. Switch v. Jones*, 555 U.S. 666 (1995).

Notice that we give the date of decision for both cites, because the decisions were in different years. Had they been in the same year (1995), then we would only give the year of decision in the second court and date parenthetical. It would look like this:

*Switch v. Bait*, 333 F.3d 444 (5th Cir.), *aff'd on other grounds sub nom. Switch v. Jones*, 555 U.S. 666 (1995).

Let's try it the other way around: cite *Switch v. Jones* with *Switch v. Bait* as *prior* history. The same explanatory phrase will not work, so go back to T.8. It looks like "*aff'g*" is what we want. Remember that we use the *-ing* form of the verb for prior history. Notice that "*aff'g*" is not followed by a comma.

*Switch v. Jones*, 555 U.S. 666 (1995), *aff'g Switch v. Bait*, 333 F.3d 444 (5th Cir. 1994).

Now, let's cite the federal district court case *Bait v. Switch* with all its subsequent history. Remember that Rule 10.7.1(a) tells you to append consecutive prior or subsequent histories to one another, separating them with a comma. Let's assume that each court affirmed the court below it:

*Bait v. Switch*, 111 F. Supp. 222 (N.D. Tex.), *aff'd*, 333 F.3d 444 (5th Cir. 1994), *aff'd sub nom. Switch v. Jones*, 555 U.S. 666 (1995).

Notice that we do not include a case name for the Fifth Circuit opinion because the name is just a reversal of the cite before it (the primary cite of *Bait v. Switch*). However, we do include the case name for *Switch v. Jones* because it names different parties than the lower court opinions. Notice also that we do not include the year of decision in the parenthetical for *Bait* v. Switch because the district court's decision was in the same year as the Fifth Circuit's decision.

Okay, one more twist on Messrs. Bait and Switch. Let's cite the Fifth Circuit opinion, giving both prior and subsequent history. Remember that Rule 10.7.1(a) tells us to include prior history first. Again, assume that the case was affirmed all the way up.

*Switch v. Bait*, 333 F.3d 444 (5th Cir.), *aff'g* 111 F. Supp. 222 (N.D. Tex. 1994), *aff'd sub nom. Switch v. Jones*, 555 U.S. 666 (1995).

See? You're getting the hang of it! Let's assume that Bait, Switch, and Jones never went to the Supreme Court. They only got as far as the Fifth Circuit before they got tired of the whole thing. However, a few years later a similar case did go to the Supreme Court, and the Supreme Court's opinion in that case (*Duck v. Cover*) explicitly overruled what the Fifth Circuit had to say in *Switch v. Bait*. That would be important history to note any time you cite *Switch v. Bait*. You would do that according to Rule 10.7.1(c):

*Switch v. Bait*, 333 F.3d 444 (5th Cir. 1994), *overruled by Duck v. Cover*, 777 U.S. 888 (1997).

Notice that "*overruled by*" is not followed by a comma.

Okay, now you're ready to make history on your own! Because these rules are so detailed, you may find the following checklists especially helpful in completing the exercise.

**Checklist for Subsequent Case History**

- Is there any reason not to include subsequent history?
    - The answer is yes if the subsequent history citation is . . .
        - an irrelevant denial of certiorari on a decision older than two years,
        - an irrelevant history on remand or denial of rehearing, or
        - a decision withdrawn by the deciding authority.
    - Otherwise, continue . . .
- Have you replaced the period at the end of the primary citation with a comma (remember that the history cite follows the *entire* primary cite, even if the primary cite includes explanatory or other types of parentheticals)?
- Have you introduced your citation with an italicized explanatory phrase?
- Have you verified whether you need a comma after the explanatory phrase directly from or based on the phrases in T.8?
- Do you need to include the case name in the history cite?
    - The answer is no if . . .
        - the party names are simply reversed,
        - the history cite is a denial of certiorari, or
        - the history cite is an administrative action with the same private parties.
    - Otherwise, include the case name.
- If you included a case name, have you added "*sub nom.*" to your explanatory phrase?
- If you added "*sub nom.*" to your explanatory phrase, have you omitted the comma following the explanatory phrase?
- If you included prior history in the citation as well, did you place the prior history first?
- Did you end your full citation sentence with a period?

**Checklist for Prior Case History**

- Do you need prior history at all?
    - Is the earlier case significant to the point the primary case is being cited for?
    - Does the earlier case better describe the issues than the primary case?
- Have you replaced the period at the end of the primary citation with a comma?
- Have you introduced your citation with an italicized explanatory phrase directly from or based on the phrases in T.8?
- Have you verified whether you need a comma after the explanatory phrase?
- Do you need to include the case name in the history cite?
    - The answer is no if . . .
        - the party names are simply reversed,

        - the history cite is a denial of certiorari, or
        - the history cite is an administrative action with the same private parties.
    - Otherwise, include the case name.
- If you included subsequent history in the citation as well, did you place the prior history first?
- If you have multiple prior history dispositions, have you joined them with "*and*"?
- Did you end your full citation sentence with a period?

## Exercise 10
## Prior & Subsequent Case History

Put the following information in correct *Bluebook* citation form. All cases are being cited in citation sentences in a brief to the United States Supreme Court. Although this exercise builds on the rules used in previous exercises, this exercise focuses on B5.1.5 and Rules 10.7 and 10.5(d). Unless the problem states otherwise, you should assume that case names are the same at each level of appeal. Remember that you must decide *whether* to include a history cite before you decide *how* to cite it. The first case listed in each problem is the primary citation. Remember that each case name must be italicized according to B13.

1. You want to cite Christopher Scott Emmett versus Loretta K. Kelly. This case is a January 2007 federal case from the Fourth Circuit Court of Appeals. It is reported in volume 474, page 154, of *Federal Reporter*, Third Series. The United States Supreme Court denied certiorari in October 2007. That denial is not yet published in *United States Reports* but is published in volume 128, page 1 of *Supreme Court Reporter*. You cite the case in a brief filed on August 10, 2008. The denial of certiorari has no impact on the argument you are drafting.

______________________________________________

______________________________________________

______________________________________________

2. You want to cite United States of America v. Timothy W. Omer. This case is a January 2005 federal appellate case from the Ninth Circuit Court of Appeals. It is reported in volume 395, page 287, of *Federal Reporter*, Third Series. The United States Supreme Court denied certiorari in January 2007. The denial is not yet published in *United States Reports* but is published in volume 127, page 1118 of *Supreme Court Reporter*. You cite the case in a brief filed September 10, 2008. The denial of certiorari has no impact on the argument you are drafting.

______________________________________________

______________________________________________

______________________________________________

3. You want to cite Susan Marie Parker, Petitioner, versus United States of America, Respondent. This is a 1969 federal case from the United States Court of Appeals for the Tenth Circuit. It is reported in volume 411, page 1067, of *Federal Reporter*, Second Series. The United States Supreme Court vacated this decision as being moot in a 1970 opinion reported in volume 397, page 96, of *United States Reports*.

______________________________________________

______________________________________________

______________________________________________

**4.** You want to cite Alveda King Beal versus Paramount Pictures Corporation and Eddie Murphy. This is a 1992 case from the United States District Court for the Northern District of Georgia. It is reported in volume 806, page 963, of *Federal Supplement*. In May of 1994, the Eleventh Circuit Court of Appeals reversed the district court's decision in an opinion reported in volume 20, page 454, of *Federal Reporter*, Third Series. Alveda King Beal applied for writ of certiorari that was denied by the United States Supreme Court in 1994. That denial appears in volume 513, page 1062, of *United States Reports*. You cite the case in a brief filed September 10, 2008. The denial of certiorari has no impact on the argument you are drafting.

______________________________________________

______________________________________________

______________________________________________

**5.** You want to cite the United States of America, Petitioner, versus One Parcel of Property. This is a 1992 federal appellate case from the Eighth Circuit Court of Appeals. It is reported in volume 964, page 814, of *Federal Reporter*, Second Series. The United States Supreme Court reversed the Eighth Circuit's decision in an opinion styled Richard Lyle Austin versus the United States. The Supreme Court's 1993 opinion is reported in volume 509, page 602, of *United States Reports*; in volume 113, page 2801, of *Supreme Court Reporter*; and in volume 125, page 488, of *Lawyers' Edition*, Second Series. You wish to direct your reader's attention to material appearing on page 818 of the Eighth Circuit's opinion.

______________________________________________

______________________________________________

______________________________________________

**6.** You want to cite James Alfonso Frye versus the United States. This is a December 3, 1923, case from the United States Court of Appeals, District of Columbia Circuit. It is reported in volume 239, page 1013, of *Federal Reporter*. In June of 1993, the United States Supreme Court overruled *Frye* in a case styled Jason Daubert and Eric Schuller, minor children, et al., versus Merrell Dow Pharmaceuticals, Incorporated. The Supreme Court's opinion is published in volume 509, page 579, of *United States Reports*.

______________________________________________

______________________________________________

______________________________________________

**7.** You want to cite Reed-Union Corporation versus Turtle Wax, Incorporated. This is a 1996 case from the United States Court of Appeals for the Seventh Circuit. It is reported in volume 77, page 909, of *Federal Reporter*, Third Series. The Seventh Circuit reversed the holding of the United States District Court for the Northern District of Illinois in that case. The 1995 district court opinion is reported in volume 869, page 1304, of *Federal Supplement*. The Northern District's opinion explains the issues more clearly and thoroughly than the court of appeals opinion.

______________________________________________

______________________________________________

______________________________________________

8. You want to cite United States, petitioner, versus Robert Lee Weaselhead, Jr., respondent. This 1999 Eighth Circuit Court of Appeals case is published in volume 165, page 1209, of *Federal Reporter*, Third Series. This decision affirms the 1997 decision of the United States District Court, District of Nebraska, in this case. The district court's decision is published in volume 36, page 908, of *Federal Supplement*, Second Series, and contains a much more thorough recitation of the significant facts than the Eighth Circuit's opinion.

9. You want to cite page 732 of Judge T. Blake Kennedy, Heber Kimball Cleveland, David Brigham Darger, Vergel Y. Jessop, William Chatwin, Charles F. Zitting, Edna Christensen, Theral Ray Dockstader, L.R. Stubbs, and Follis Gardner Pett, versus the United States of America, a kidnapping case. This 1945 Tenth Circuit case is published in volume 146, page 730, of *Federal Reporter*, Second Series. The Tenth Circuit affirmed the trial court decision of the District Court for Utah. The District Court's 1945 decision is published in volume 56, page 890, of *Federal Supplement* and gives the best explanation of the issues in this case. Following the decision in this case by the Tenth Circuit, the Supreme Court heard this case and reversed the Tenth Circuit in a 1946 opinion reported in volume 326, page 455, of *United States Reports*.

10. You want to cite Robert Johnson Mayes, plaintiff-petitioner, versus James Marshall Pickett, Warden, defendant-respondent. This is a 1976 opinion from the Ninth Circuit Court of Appeals. It is reported in volume 537, page 1080, of *Federal Reporter*, Second Series. The United States Supreme Court dismissed certiorari for this case on September 27, 1976. This dismissal is published in volume 434, page 801, of *United States Reports*. The Supreme Court subsequently denied certiorari on May 16, 1977. The denial was reported under the name of United States v. Robert Johnson Mayes in volume 435, page 924, of *United States Reports*. Both the dismissal and the denial were related to issues for which you intend to cite the Ninth Circuit opinion.

# Chapter 11
# TEXAS COURTS OF APPEALS CASES

Citation to cases from Texas intermediate courts of appeals uses rules created outside of *The Bluebook*. Those additional rules are found in Chapter 4 of *Texas Rules of Form* (currently in its Eleventh Edition). These rules govern the information to be included in the court and date parenthetical and to be included as subsequent history. You should read Chapter 4 in *Texas Rules of Form* before continuing. You may also want to refer to those rules as they are mentioned and explained in this chapter.

## A. Court & Date Parenthetical

Rules 4.1.1 and 4.3.1 tell you that the court and date parenthetical for Texas intermediate courts of appeals cases includes a designation indicating that the case is a court of appeals case (*i.e.*, Tex. App.) and another indicating the location of the court (*e.g.*, Austin). (See Rules 4.1.1 and 4.3.1 for examples.)

Between 1911 and August 31, 1981, Texas intermediate courts of appeals had only civil jurisdiction. For cases decided during that time, Rule 4.2.1 requires that the court designation be abbreviated as "Tex. Civ. App." Beginning September 1, 1981, those courts acquired and continue to have criminal jurisdiction. For cases decided on and after that date, Rule 4.1.1 requires that the court designation be abbreviated as "Tex. App."

In addition to the designation "Tex. Civ. App." or "Tex. App.," the court is also identified by its location. Rule 4.3.1 lists the cities in which the courts of appeals are located. The numbers in that list correspond to the district numbers of the courts of appeals. For example, the Seventh District Court of Appeals is seventh on the list. That court sits in Amarillo. Notice that both the First and Fourteenth Districts sit in Houston. To distinguish them in citations, the district number in brackets follows the city name. (See the examples in Rule 4.3.1.) Houston courts of appeals are the only courts that take a district number designation in the parenthetical.

Notice the spaces between each abbreviation in both "Tex. Civ. App." and "Tex. App." Notice also that no space is placed before or after the em dash [1] that separates the court designation from the city.

## B. History

Rule 4.4 also tells us that we must include writ history, petition history, or other subsequent history for intermediate courts of appeals cases. This is especially important because the writ and subsequent history notations give the reader important information about the weight of the authority. (See Appendices D & E of *Texas Rules of Form*.) Although you would only note a denial of certiorari by the United States Supreme Court in certain situations, you will always include writ and petition history for Texas state courts of appeals.

---

[1] An em dash (—) looks like an extra long hyphen (-). If you cannot produce an em dash, then use two hyphens (--). On most current versions of word processors, after you type two hyphens in a row, they will automatically be combined into an em dash.

### 1. History Without an Opinion

Writ and petition history notations tell the reader whether either of the two highest courts in Texas, the Texas Supreme Court and Texas Court of Criminal Appeals, has been asked by a party in a writ or petition to dispose of the cited case. If the Supreme Court or Court of Criminal Appeals has disposed of a writ or petition without an opinion, we give writ or petition history *inside* the court and date parenthetical following the year of decision according to the rules below. The history notation inside the parenthetical is **not italicized.**

> *Cochran v. Shannon*, 456 S.W.2d 789 (Tex. App.—Amarillo 2000, pet. denied).

If one of those courts has issued an opinion in disposing of the writ or petition, we give subsequent history *following* the court and date parenthetical according to the rules in the following section, *2. History With an Opinion*, and Rule 4.6.1(b). The history notation following the parenthetical in that situation **is italicized.**

> *Cochran v. Shannon*, 456 S.W.2d 789 (Tex. App.—Amarillo 2000), *pet. denied*, 458 S.W.2d 321 (Tex. 2001).

Civil cases have either writ or petition history, depending on the date the request for review was filed. Before September 1, 1997, parties attempting to appeal a civil case filed a "writ"; so filings before that date created "writ history." These writ history notations are found in Rule 4.4.2. Beginning September 1, 1997, that same "writ" has been called a "petition," thus creating "petition history." The civil petition history notations are found in Rule 4.4.1.

Because parties to criminal cases have always filed a "petition" for review, criminal cases have only petition history, regardless of the date of decision. Those criminal petition history notations are found in Rule 4.5.

The source we use to find the history of a case is the *Texas Subsequent History Table*. The table is arranged in order of the volumes of *South Western Reporter*, beginning with volume 20, and each page looks similar to a page in a bound volume of a Shepard's citator. Each page contains four columns. Each column contains notations that indicate which volume of *South Western Reporter* is covered by that portion of the column (for example, one such notation might be "232 S.W.2d," indicating that everything below it is in volume 232 of *South Western Reporter*, Second Series). The numbers below the volume designations correspond to page numbers within that volume. The notations beside each page number give the disposition of that case. You will no doubt soon notice that the abbreviations in the table are different from the abbreviations in Rules 4.4.1, 4.4.2, and 4.5. Always use the disposition abbreviations given in *Texas Rules of Form* rather than relying on the abbreviations in the *Texas Subsequent History Table*. [2]

This table is updated in the advance sheets of *South Western Reporter*, Texas Cases Offprint. Therefore, cases too recent to be listed in the current edition of the table should appear in the most recent advance sheets.

If no notation appears for a case, then we assume that neither party has filed a petition; we may note this fact by using either "no pet. h." or "no pet." These two notations are the most commonly confused, but each has a distinct meaning. Use

---

[2] Warning! Warning! You may now be using electronic databases, such as LexisNexis and WESTLAW. Each source has products that tell you about procedural history of cases, including the status of petitions. The language and abbreviations used, however, do not always follow the phrases used by Texas Rules of Form. When citing Texas Courts of Appeals cases to Texas courts, always remember to use the abbreviated phrases in Texas Rules of Form rather than relying on the online abbreviation.

"no pet. h." during the time period that a petition may be filed and pending. Many practitioners use a rule of thumb of two years. Therefore, if your citation is less than two years old, and you find no information in the *Subsequent History Table*, use the notation "no pet. h." That indicates to your reader that, at this point, all you know for sure is that no petition *history* has been recorded. This leaves open the possibility that a petition may have been filed. However, if more than two years have passed and you find no information in the *Subsequent History Table*, it is unlikely that a petition was ever filed, so you would use the notation "no pet." to indicate that no petition was ever filed.

### 2. History With an Opinion

If the Texas Supreme Court or Court of Criminal Appeals issues an opinion in a case, either after the petition or writ is granted or in otherwise disposing of the petition or writ, that information should be given as subsequent history according to Rule 4.6.1.

You will know that the court has issued an opinion by the notation in the *Subsequent History Table*. Rather than a history notation, a citation to another case will appear next to your page number. You will have to look up that citation to find out how the high court disposed of your intermediate court of appeals case.

If the citation is to an opinion issued in conjunction with the granting or refusal of a request for review, you will indicate the disposition (found in Rules 4.4.1, 4.4.2, or 4.5) in italics after the court and date parenthetical followed by the citation to the case.

*Cochran v. Shannon*, 456 S.W.2d 789 (Tex. App.—Amarillo 2000), *pet. denied*, 458 S.W.2d 321 (Tex. 2001).

If the citation is to an opinion the court issued after granting the request for review and deciding the case, you will include this citation as subsequent history just as you learned in the Prior & Subsequent History exercise.

*Cochran v. Shannon*, 456 S.W.2d 789 (Tex. App.—Amarillo 2000), *aff'd*, 458 S.W.2d 321 (Tex. 2001).

## C. Memorandum Opinions & Opinions Not Designated for Publication

Finally, the citation may need an additional parenthetical if it is a memorandum opinion or an opinion not designated for publication. [3] (See the examples in Rule 4.1.2.) If the opinion is simply designated as an opinion for publication, no parenthetical is necessary.

## D. Dry Run

Whew! Got all that? It's really less complicated than it might seem. Let's try one. Say that you want to cite *Robbins v. Hng Oil Co.* The opinion was issued by the Fourteenth District Court of Appeals in Houston in 1994. The opinion is printed in volume 878 of *South Western Reporter*, Second Series, page 351. First, get down the information you already know from completing past ICW exercises:

*Robbins v. Hng Oil Co.*, 878 S.W.2d 351

The first decision you have to make is whether to call the court "Tex. Civ. App." or "Tex. App." Because this case would have been filed well after August 31, 1981,

[3] Why the court might designate an opinion as a memorandum opinion after January 1, 2003, and why a prior opinion might not be designated for publication are beyond the scope of the ICW. Your professor will likely cover this.

when the courts of appeals acquired criminal jurisdiction, we will refer to the court as "Tex. App."

*Robbins v. Hng Oil Co.*, 878 S.W.2d 351 (Tex. App.

Next, add the city of the court. It will be separated from "Tex. App." by an em dash, or two hyphens, with no spaces before or after:

*Robbins v. Hng Oil Co.*, 878 S.W.2d 351 (Tex. App.—Houston

Because this is a Houston court of appeals case, you will also need to include the district number in brackets. Remember that only cites to Houston courts of appeals cases include the district number—all other courts are sufficiently identified by the name of the city.

*Robbins v. Hng Oil Co.*, 878 S.W.2d 351 (Tex. App.—Houston [14th Dist.]

Then add the year of decision:

*Robbins v. Hng Oil Co.*, 878 S.W.2d 351 (Tex. App.—Houston [14th Dist.] 1994

Now that you are done with the court and date information, you need to add the writ history (notice that you will have writ history rather than petition history because this case was decided before September 1, 1997, when civil cases began to have petition history). For that, you will need to go to the *Texas Subsequent History Table.* First, find the page that contains all the cases in volume 878. Then see if there is a notation for page 351. Going down the list, you see the notation "Dism. w.o.j." next to the number 351. Remembering that you cannot rely on the abbreviations in the table, you look back at Rule 4.4.1 for the list of writ history notations. You see that the sixth notation contains your match: "writ dism'd w.o.j." So add it to your citation, separating it from the court and date information with a comma. Finally, close the parentheses and end your citation sentence with a period. Hey, that wasn't so hard!

*Robbins v. Hng Oil Co.*, 878 S.W.2d 351 (Tex. App.—Houston [14th Dist.] 1994, writ dism'd. w.o.j.).

Now let's assume than when you looked up page 351 under the column notation "878 S.W.2d," you did not find an abbreviation for subsequent history. Instead, you found a notation that looks like this: 880 SW2d 125. First, you would go to the shelves in the library containing *South Western Reporter*, Second Series, and look up page 125 of volume 880. You would discover that the Supreme Court had issued an opinion in 1994 that explained why it had dismissed the writ for want of jurisdiction. In that situation, your citation would look like this:

*Robbins v. Hng Oil Co.*, 878 S.W.2d 351 (Tex. App.—Houston [14th Dist.]), *writ dism'd w.o.j.*, 880 S.W.2d 125 (Tex. 1994). [4]

How about one final twist? What if you had found that same citation next to page 351 just as in the example above; but when you went to look it up, you found that the Supreme Court had granted the request for review, heard the case, and then issued an opinion reversing the Fourteenth Court of Appeals' decision? In that situation, your citation would look like this:

*Robbins v. Hng Oil Co.*, 878 S.W.2d 351 (Tex. App.—Houston [14th Dist.]), *rev'd*, 880 S.W.2d 125 (Tex. 1994).

---

[4] Here is a little prior and subsequent history review: Remember that you omit the first date of decision when the subsequent citation is from the same year.

Finally, assume that instead of going up for review by the Texas Supreme Court, the parties decided not to pursue the case beyond the Court of Appeals and that the court designated its opinion as a memorandum opinion. In that case, the citation would look like this:

> *Robbins v. Hng Oil Co.*, 878 S.W.2d 351 (Tex. App.—Houston [14th Dist.] 1994, no pet.) (mem. op.).

Okay, now that you've got it, it's time to do some citin' TEXAS STYLE!

## Checklist for Texas Courts of Appeals Cases

- Is your case an intermediate courts of appeals case from Texas? If not, you don't need *Texas Rules of Form*. Back to *The Bluebook* with you!
- Was your opinion issued on or before August 31, 1981?
  - If so, then the court designation is "Tex. Civ. App."
  - If not, then the court designation is "Tex. App."
- Have you identified the city in which the court is located, being sure to leave no spaces before or after the separating dash?
- If you have a Houston court of appeals case, have you identified the district in brackets?
- Have you looked up the case in the *Texas Subsequent History Table*?
  - If you did not find a notation, has the time expired for filing a request for review?
    - If yes, use the notation "no pet."
    - If no, use the notation "no pet. h."
  - If you found a history notation . . .
    - have you made sure that you use the appropriate abbreviation from Rule 4.4.1, 4.4.2, or 4.5?
    - did you place the history notation **unitalicized** within the court and date parenthetical?
  - If you found a citation to another case . . .
    - did you lock the case up?
    - if it was an opinion explaining why the court granted or refused the request for review, have you used the appropriate abbreviation from Rule 4.4.1, 4.4.2, or 4.5?
    - if it was an opinion issued after the court granted review and heard the case, have you appropriately noted the subsequent history according to Rule 10.7 and T.8 of *The Bluebook*?
    - did you place the history notation outside the court and date parenthetical and italicize it?
- Did you remember to end your citation sentence with a period?

## Exercise 11
## Texas Courts Of Appeals Cases

Put the following information in correct *Bluebook* and *Texas Rules of Form* citation form. All cases are being cited in citation sentences to the Texas Supreme Court. Although this exercise builds on the rules used in the previous exercises, this exercise focuses on Texas Rules of Form, Chapter 4. For each question, you must use the correct typeface given in B13 and the correct spacing given in Rule 6.1. You will need to look up the history for each case in the most current *Texas Subsequent History Table*. You may need to locate the cases cited in the history for additional information about the disposition.

1. Midland National Life Insurance Company, successor to Reserve Life Insurance Company, Appellant, versus Arlie Bridges, Appellee. This 1994 case is from the Eastland Court of Appeals. It is reported in volume 889, page 17, of *South Western Reporter*, Second Series.

______________________________________________

______________________________________________

______________________________________________

2. Shirley Robinson, Appellant, versus Warner-Lambert Pharmaceuticals Company and Old Corner Drug, Appellees. This 1999 case is from the Tenth District Court of Appeals. It is reported in volume 998, page 407, of *South Western Reporter*, Second Series.

______________________________________________

______________________________________________

______________________________________________

3. Ivan Jones, et al., Appellants, versus Beech Aircraft Corporation, Appellee. This 1999 case is from the San Antonio Court of Appeals. It is reported in volume 995, page 767, of *South Western Reporter*, Second Series.

______________________________________________

______________________________________________

______________________________________________

4. American National Insurance Company, versus Doug Savage, et al. This 1937 case is from the San Antonio Court of Appeals. It is reported in volume 112, page 240, of *South Western Reporter*, Second Series.

______________________________________________

______________________________________________

______________________________________________

5. Bristol-Myers Squibb Company, Surgitek, Incorporated, and Medical Engineering Corporation, Appellants, versus Tonya Lynne Goldston and Foy Goldston, et al., Appellees. This is a 1998 case from the Second District Court of Appeals. It is reported in volume 983, page 369, of *South Western Reporter*, Second Series.

______________________________________________

______________________________________________

______________________________________________

6. Lawrence Edward Speth, Appellant, versus The State of Texas, Appellee. This is a 1997 criminal case from the Houston Court of Appeals, Fourteenth District. It is reported in volume 939, page 769, of *South Western Reporter*, Second Series.

_______________________________________________

_______________________________________________

_______________________________________________

7. Tanja Hernandez, Appellant, versus The State of Texas, Appellee. This is a 1999 criminal case from the Third District Court of Appeals. It is reported in volume 986, page 817, of *South Western Reporter*, Second Series.

_______________________________________________

_______________________________________________

_______________________________________________

8. Tidewater Associated Oil Co., et al., versus J.K. Hughes Oil Company, et al. This is a 1952 case from the Austin Court of Appeals. It is reported in volume 250, page 405, of *South Western Reporter*, Second Series.

_______________________________________________

_______________________________________________

_______________________________________________

9. James A. Green, Jr., et al., Appellants, versus A.K. Meadows, Appellee. This is a 1974 case from the Houston Court of Appeals, First District. It is reported in volume 517, page 799, of *South Western Reporter*, Second Series.

_______________________________________________

_______________________________________________

_______________________________________________

10. Donna Renae Russell, Appellant, versus The State of Texas, Appellee. This is a 1987 criminal case from the Dallas Court of Appeals. It is reported in volume 739, page 923, of *South Western Reporter*, Second Series.

_______________________________________________

_______________________________________________

_______________________________________________

# Chapter 12
# SECONDARY SOURCES

By now, you are highly proficient in citing any type of case law or legislative enactment. But you may want to cite to information located in other sources such as books, law reviews, and periodicals. You may even find yourself needing to cite to something more esoteric like a letter, a telephone interview, or an unpublished working paper. *The Bluebook* even has rules for citing to sources such as these in their original media. Because you are already proficient in citing sources of positive law, citing these other print sources will be a snap.

However, you may be doing more and more of this type of research over the Internet or through an electronic database. Chapter 16 will explore how to cite sources found through these types of research. This chapter will focus on citing the original print source. Rule 15 governs books and pamphlets; Rule 16, periodical materials; and Rule 17, unpublished and forthcoming publications. B8 covers the citation of all these sources in legal documents and office memoranda. Please review these rules before attempting Exercise 12.

### A. Books

First, you will notice that Rule 15 requires both the author's name and the title to appear in LARGE AND SMALL CAPITALS. However, B13 provides instead that in legal memoranda and court documents, we italicize the title of books and that authors' names appear in plain type. The basic citation form for a book, however, is the same as shown at the beginning of Rule 15. The basic book citation will contain information regarding:

- the full name of the author or authors,
- the title of the book,
- the editor and/or translator, if any, and
- the date.

If you would like to send your reader to a specific page or pages in the book, the page number would immediately follow the title.

Author, *Title* Pg. (Editor, Date).

Rule 15.1 tells you to give the author's name just as it appears. Unlike other citation systems you may have learned in your undergraduate or graduate studies, you do not rewrite the name to put the surname first. If the book has two authors, include both names joined by an ampersand (&) in the order that the names appear in the book.

Jonathan Harr, *A Civil Action* (1997).

Burton Silver & Heather Busch, *Dancing with Cats* (1999).

However, if the book has more than two authors, you may include the name of only the first author immediately followed by the words "et al."

J. Myron Jacobstein et al., *Fundamentals of Legal Research* 121 (6th ed. 1994).

Notice that Rule 15.1(b) tells you that you may list more than two authors by name when the inclusion of other authors is "particularly relevant." Whether an author is particularly relevant depends on whether knowing of the author's participation will help the reader better understand the weight or substance of the source. Fame alone does not make an author "particularly relevant."

The next piece of information that your reader will need after the author is the title of the work. You should include the full title as it appears on the title page. Do not alter the title by abbreviating or omitting words, but capitalize according to Rule 8, which tells you to capitalize all words except articles, conjunctions, and prepositions of four or fewer letters. Rule 8 also tells us to always capitalize the first word in a title and the first word following a colon.

Paul Alexander, *Salinger: A Biography* (1999).

Remember, the overriding concern in legal citation is that the reader should have enough information to find the exact source that you are citing. Therefore, if the book has many editions or translations, you will need to include the editor or translator. The name of an editor will be followed immediately by the abbreviation "ed." and the name of a translator will be followed immediately by the abbreviation "trans." The abbreviations for "editor," "translator," and similar publishing terms appear in T.14. If a book has two editors or translators, then both names will appear and be followed immediately by "eds." or "trans." respectively. The naming of editors and translators follows the same rule as the naming of authors; if a book has more than two editors or translators, then you may include the name of only the first editor or translator followed by "et al." Editor and translator information appears in the date parenthetical.

Gabriel Garcia Marquez, *Love in the Time of Cholera* 69-70 (Edith Grossman trans., 1988).

Sometimes, a book will not have a specific author, only an editor. In this situation, no author information will appear, and the editor information will appear in the date parenthetical.

*The Antarctic Treaty Regime* (Gillian D. Triggs ed., 1987).

The last piece of information you must include is the date of publication. Many books have only one publication date. However, some books are published in several editions, sometimes by the same publisher and sometimes by different publishers. If only one publisher has published a book, then you include only the number of the edition and the year the edition was published in the date parenthetical. (Always cite to the latest edition.) This information is necessary for your reader to be able to consult a source that you are citing by page number. The page numbers of various editions will not be consistent, so your reader will need to know exactly what edition you are citing.

J. Myron Jacobstein et al., *Fundamentals of Legal Research* 121 (6th ed. 1994).

However, if more than one publisher has published the book, then you must indicate the name of the editor, if any, the name of the publisher, and the date of publication of the edition you are citing. If the publisher has published several editions of the work, you will also need to include the edition. You will also include in a separate parenthetical the original date of publication, unless the work is regularly updated or revised. For example, if you are citing a work of literature, you would include in the date parenthetical the name of the publisher and the date of the edition that you are citing. You would also include the original publication date in a separate parenthetical because the actual book is not being updated or revised.

Thomas Hardy, *Tess of the D'Urbervilles* (David Skelton ed., Penguin Books 1978) (1891).

## B. Collections

Many books that you will cite will be collections of articles or essays. These sources follow the rule for shorter works in collection, Rule 15.5. In your legal citation, you must include:

- the full name of the author of the specific work that you are citing,
- the title of the specific work,
- the title of the collection,
- the page number on which the specific work appears,
- the editor, if any, and
- the date.

Author, *Work Title, in Collection Title* Pg. (Editor, Date)

Although Rule 15.5.1 provides that the name of the specific work appears in italics and the name of the collection in large and small capitals, B8 modifies that rule and tells us to italicize the titles of both. The name of the author appears in ordinary roman type, regardless of whether the author wrote all of the works in the collection.

> Anthony A. Peacock, *Strange Brew: Tocqueville, Rights, and the Technology of Equality, in Rethinking the Constitution: Perspectives on Canadian Constitutional Reform, Interpretation, and Theory* 122, 125–56 (Anthony A. Peacock ed., 1996).

In addition, some frequently cited books have special citation forms. Rule 15.8 gives you the citation forms for *The Bible*, *The Federalist*, the *Manual* for Complex Litigation, plays written by William Shakespeare, and other frequently cited works.

## C. Periodicals

You will also on occasion cite to articles in periodicals and law reviews. Rule 16 provides the rules on citing to periodical materials. B9 tells you that the name of the author should appear in ordinary roman type, the title of the article should be italicized, and the title of the publication should appear in ordinary roman type. This instruction overrides the typeface conventions given in Rule 16, which tell you to put titles of periodicals in large and small capitals. The basic form is similar to the form used for shorter works in a collection. In your legal citation, you must include

- the full name of the author of the article that you are citing,
- the title of the article,
- the title of the publication and any other pertinent volume or series information,
- the page number on which the specific work appears, and
- the date.

This information will appear in your legal citation differently depending on whether your source is a "consecutively paginated journal" or a "nonconsecutively paginated journal."

### 1. Consecutively Paginated Journals

Rule 16.3 governs consecutively paginated journals. The most common consecutively paginated journal you will use is a law review. Law reviews are organized by volumes, which generally correspond to an academic year. However, each "volume" may be printed in separately bound publications with edition numbers. For example, Volume 22 of a certain law review may actually span three separately bound publications, which are usually soft-bound editions. Each publication may be given a number: Volume 22, No. 2. Once a volume is complete, the soft-bound numbered editions are collected and permanently bound as one volume. Therefore, the pages in each publication are numbered beginning with page 1 in Volume 22, No. 1 and ending with the last page of Volume 22, No. 3. Because of this numbering system, only the volume number and the page number are necessary to point your reader to the correct publication.

Author, *Article*, Vol. Periodical Pg. (Date)

Stephen R. Heifetz, *Blue in the Face: The Bluebook, the Bar Exam, and the Paradox of Our Legal Culture*, 51 Rutgers L. Rev. 695 (1999).

**2. Nonconsecutively Paginated Journals**

You may also need to cite to a nonconsecutively paginated journal, such as a magazine. Rule 16.4 governs nonconsecutively paginated journals. The format is generally the same as above, but without a volume designation. Instead, you will include the full date of publication before the page number on which the article cited appears. This information will enable your reader to find a specific issue of a nonconsecutively paginated journal. Note that *The Bluebook* has its own abbreviations for months of the year in T.12. The page number follows the word "at."

Author, *Article*, Periodical, Full Date, at Pg.

Samantha Miller & Dan Jewel, *Brat Race*, People, Apr. 19, 1999, at 114.

Notice that you never put the title of the article in quotation marks. Also note that when citing to any periodical, however paginated, you must consult T.13, which lists abbreviations for common legal periodicals and for words commonly used in periodical titles, and also T.10, which lists abbreviations for geographical regions. Rule 16.4 tells you to use these Tables to abbreviate the title of the cited periodical.

**3. Newspapers**

The other type of periodical that you may refer to in your legal writing is a newspaper. Rule 16.5 governs newspapers. The format is the same for nonconsecutively paginated journals. If the newspaper article does not name an author, then you simply omit any author information. Again, P.1(b) tells you that the title of the article is italicized, but the title of the periodical and the name of the author appear in plain type.

Author, *Article*, Periodical, Full Date, at Pg.

Edmund L. Andrews, *Total Fina Is Victorious with Bid for Elf Acquitaine*, N.Y. Times, Sept. 14, 1999, at C1.

Rule 16.6 governs the specialized formats for less common sources, such as student-written law review materials, book reviews, newsletters and symposia.

### D. Nonprint Sources

On the occasions you will need to cite to a source that is unpublished in a written medium, Rule 17 covers these types of sources. Even speeches, interviews, and letters are covered here. In this age of electronic access to working papers via the Social Science Research Network (SSRN) and the National Bureau of Economic Research, new Rule 17.3 tells us how to cite to these forthcoming works.

## Exercise 12
## Secondary Sources

Put the following information in correct *Bluebook* citation form. All sources are being cited in citation sentences. Although this exercise builds on the rules used in the previous exercise, this exercise focuses on Rules 15, 16, and 17 and B8 and B9. You should follow the convention of placing one space after a colon, period, or question mark within a title.

1. "The Tempting of America," a book published in 1990 by Simon & Schuster Inc. in New York. The author is Robert H. Bork. You want to focus your reader's attention on page 6.

___

___

___

2. "Getting to Maybe: How to Excel on Law School Exams," a book by Richard Michael Fischl and Jeremy Paul, published in 1999 by Carolina Academic Press in Durham, North Carolina.

___

___

___

3. An article by A. Darby Dickerson entitled "An Un-Uniform System of Citation: Surviving with the New Bluebook," published beginning on page 53 of volume 26 of the Stetson Law Review in 1996.

___

___

___

4. "The Mayor of Casterbridge," a novel written by Thomas Hardy in 1885. You are citing to a paperback version published in 1994 by Bantam Classics in New York.

___

___

___

5. "Facing the Music," an article by John Gibeaut, published in the October 2000 issue of the *ABA Journal*. The article appears on 37.

___

___

___

6. A newspaper article by Linda Greenhouse entitled "Court Takes Case Testing the Limits of Vouchers Laws." This article appeared at A1 of the New York Times on Wednesday, September 26, 2001.

___

___

___

7. An article by Catharine A. MacKinnon entitled "Vindication and Resistance: A Response to the Carnegie Mellon Study of Pornography in Cyberspace." This 1995 article appeared in volume 83 of the George Washington Law Review beginning on page 1959. You wish to direct your reader's attention to page 1963 of this article.

________________________________________________

________________________________________________

________________________________________________

8. An introduction written by Jan Richard Schlichtmann to "A Documentary Companion to *A Civil Action*," written by Lewis A. Grossman and Robert G. Vaughn. The introduction appears on page xxvi. The book was published in 1999 by Foundation Press.

________________________________________________

________________________________________________

________________________________________________

9. "Enron's Power Crisis," an article by Bethany McLean in the September 17, 2001 edition of *Fortune* magazine. The article begins on page 48.

________________________________________________

________________________________________________

________________________________________________

10. "Impeach the Supremes," an article by David Sarasohn in the August 20, 2001 edition of *The Nation*. The article begins on page 4.

________________________________________________

________________________________________________

________________________________________________

11. An essay entitled "The Economic Approach to Homosexuality," by Richard A. Posner, which appears on page 173 of the larger collection, "Sex, Preference, and Family." This work was published in 1997 by Oxford University Press in New York. The editors of the work are David M. Estlund and Martha C. Nussbaum.

________________________________________________

________________________________________________

________________________________________________

12. An article by Michael D. Weiss entitled "Actually Shutting Down the Virtual Multistate Corporation." This article was published in volume 28 of the Indiana Law Review beginning on page 607 in 1995.

________________________________________________

________________________________________________

________________________________________________

# Chapter 13

# PARENTHETICALS

We know that legal citation serves two primary purposes: to give attribution to a source and to give locating information for a source. In addition, you have probably learned in your legal writing course that citations can also help make your writing more concise. Your citation can minimize or eliminate the need for some detailed explanation. For example, citations can give the year of decision and the jurisdiction of the case so that you do not have to give that information textually.

Instead of:

> In 1995, the Texas Supreme Court held that false imprisonment is the willful detention of another without that person's consent and without authority of law. *Randall's Food Mkts., Inc. v. Johnson*, 891 S.W.2d 640 (Tex. 1995).

You can write:

> False imprisonment is the willful detention of another without that person's consent and without authority of law. *Randall's Food Mkts., Inc. v. Johnson*, 891 S.W.2d 640 (Tex. 1995).

Citation parentheticals and signals provide additional citation tools for giving your reader useful information without including that information in a detailed discussion. In this chapter, you will learn how to use parentheticals. In the next chapter, you will learn how to use signals, both alone and in conjunction with parentheticals.

*The Bluebook* quick reference for parentheticals is in B5.1.4 and B11 of the Bluepages. Read these sections before continuing.

You have probably noticed in your legal reading that a great deal of information of several kinds is enclosed in parentheses at the end of some citations. This information falls generally into two categories: weight of authority and explanation. Weight of authority parentheticals give the reader information that indicates the precedential value of a cited case.

> *Welsh v. United States*, 398 U.S. 333 (1970) **(plurality opinion).** [1]

Explanatory parentheticals provide additional information to make clear to the reader the reason for the citation.

> *In re Marriage of Wood*, 567 N.W.2d 680 (Iowa Ct. App. 1997) **(upholding an order modifying child support and requiring the father to contribute toward college expenses of the children).**

While weight of authority parentheticals are only used with case citations, explanatory parentheticals may be used with any type of authority cited.

### A. Weight of Authority Parentheticals

Rule 10.6.1 explains how the case's precedential value should be included in a citation. Generally, two types of information indicate that the case does not have the

---

[1] Information appears in bold print for highlighting purposes only. You should not format any part of your citation in bold print.

same value as other cases decided by the same court — information that indicates the weight of the authority (*e.g.*, en banc, per curiam, unpublished table decision) and information that shows that the proposition cited is not the clear holding of the majority of the court (*e.g.*, 5-4 decision, dissenting opinion, dictum). For example, a case decided by a single Supreme Court justice sitting as a circuit justice has less precedential value than one decided by the entire Court. In that case, T.1 (Federal section, Circuit Justice subsection) gives the format for that parenthetical:

(Scalia, Circuit Justice)

Similarly, a quotation of text from a dissenting opinion would not have the same weight as a quotation from the majority opinion. In that case, the parenthetical would look like this:

*TXO Prod. Corp. v. Alliance Res. Corp.*, 509 U.S. 443, 473 (1993) **(O'Connor, J., dissenting).**

The page numbers given are only those for the initial page of the case and the page for the specific material cited. Those are the only page numbers needed because Rule 3.2(a) tells us *not* to include the initial page number of concurring or dissenting opinions.

In drafting weight of authority parentheticals, be guided by the examples in Rule 10.6.1.

### B. Explanatory Parentheticals

Legal writers sometimes include information in explanatory parentheticals to citations to provide additional information that makes clear to the reader the relevance of the citation. Parentheticals provide a clear, concise, economical means of getting the maximum information to the reader with a minimum of detailed explanation. Their use is especially helpful when the writer does not really want to discuss the parenthetical information in text but still considers it necessary to help the reader fit the citation into the overall picture.

Rule 1.5 gives the general rules for the mechanics of including explanatory parentheticals in citations to cases, statutes, and secondary sources. Rule 1.6(c) supplements Rule 1.5 with specific guidance for giving commentary in an explanatory parenthetical. Rule 12.7 gives specific rules for using explanatory parentheticals with statutes. B.11 is a good general guide on when and how to use explanatory parentheticals. The following discussion is applicable to all types of authority.

Most often, explanatory phrases begin with the present participle form of a verb (one that ends in *-ing*).

W. Wendell Hall, *Standards of Review in Texas*, 29 St. Mary's L.J. 351, 354 (1998) (**explaining** the difference between the standards of review for "no evidence" and "insufficient evidence").

Because the explanation is a phrase, it does not need a period within the parentheses.

Commentary phrases governed by Rule 1.6(c) and 10.6.2 also begin with *-ing* verbs.[2] Commentary explains how the authority cited is related to the authority in the parenthetical.

La. Civ. Code Ann. arts. 2317, 2322 (West 1979) (**codifying** the rule in

---

[2] Explanatory words inside a parenthetical generally are not italicized. Therefore, words like "citing" and "quoting" should not be italicized in an explanatory parenthetical. This is consistent with the examples in the Bluebook. *Bluepages Rule B13 instructs that "citing" should be italicized. This is an error.* The phrase "cited in" — but not "citing" — should be italicized as per Rule 1.6(c).

*Coulter v. Texaco, Inc.*, 547 F.2d 909, 913 (5th Cir. 1977)).

*Meeker v. Hamilton Grain Elevator Co.*, 442 N.E.2d 922 (Ill. 1982) (**quoting** *Bonebrake v. Cox*, 499 F.2d 951 (8th Cir. 1974)).

If the context of the citation makes a participial phrase unnecessary, a shorter phrase may be used:

The interviewer may be anyone authorized to investigate employment matters. *See e.g.*, *Black v. Kroger Co.*, 527 S.W.2d 794 (Tex. Civ. App.—Houston [14th Dist.] 1975, no writ) **(store manager)**; *Safeway Stores, Inc. v. Amburn*, 388 S.W.2d 443 (Tex. Civ. App.—Fort Worth 1965, no writ) **(security guard employed by Safeway)**.

### C. Order of Parentheticals

Because case citations may include both weight of authority parentheticals and explanatory parentheticals, legal writers need a rule to guide them in ordering multiple parentheticals. Rule 10.6.3 requires that writers list weight of authority parentheticals before explanatory parentheticals and that both follow the court and date parenthetical of the cited case.

*O'Connor v. Bd. of Educ.*, 449 U.S. 1301, 1306 (1980) **(Stevens, J., concurring) (affirming an order vacating a temporary injunction)**.

If the citation also includes prior or subsequent history, the parenthetical should follow the court and date parenthetical of the primary cited case rather than following the last case in the citation.

*Bennett v. Plenert*, 63 F.3d 915 (5th Cir. 1995) **(holding that ranchers and irrigation districts were not within zone of interests protected by ESA)**, *rev'd on other grounds*, 520 U.S. 154 (1997).

Mastery of the art of drafting explanatory parenthetical phrases will help you become a polished, professional legal writer — one who gets his or her point across in the fewest possible words. With a few well-chosen words in a parenthetical phrase, you will be able to communicate the crux of a case or other authority without discussing it at all in text.

### D. Dry Run

Let's walk through the process of figuring out (1) whether a citation needs a parenthetical and (2) if it does, how to put it together.

Suppose we want to cite *Smith v. Brown*, 123 U.S. 456, 467 (1970). We are citing Justice Euclid's concurring opinion. Concurrences do not have the same precedential value as majority opinions. Accordingly, Rule 10.6.1 indicates that we need a parenthetical phrase because the proposition for which it is cited is "not the single, clear holding of a majority of the court." The examples show that we should convey the appropriate weight of authority by adding the following weight of authority parenthetical after the basic citation:

(Euclid, J., concurring).

Although this is a well-known case, we wish to cite it for one of its lesser-known propositions. Therefore, Rule 1.5 and B11 recommend an explanatory parenthetical to make the citation's relevance clear.

So we must decide what to say and how to say it in the parenthetical. We are citing page 467 of the case on which Justice Euclid says in dicta that if X were Y, the jury's verdict would not have been allowed to stand. In our brief, we are arguing that the general rule represented by *Smith v. Brown* should not apply to our client's case because, on our facts, X *is* probably Y. How can we word that in an explanatory parenthetical so that it will be clear and concise?

First, the parenthetical phrase should begin with a present participle verb. We cannot use "holding" because the statement was dicta and appeared in a concurring opinion. Instead, we could use "suggesting" for our first word. For the rest, we can simply say "that if X were Y, the jury's verdict would not have been allowed to stand." Although we could quote the court's language in our parenthetical, the better practice is to paraphrase unless the actual words of the court are particularly memorable or concise.

Finally we must decide in what order to put the parenthetical phrases. Rule 10.6.3 guides us here. The weight of authority parenthetical must precede the explanatory parenthetical. So the completed citation would look like this:

> *Smith v. Brown*, 123 U.S. 456, 467 (1970) (Euclid, J., concurring) (suggesting that if X were Y, the jury's verdict would not have been allowed to stand).

Notice the one space between each set of parentheses and the period at the end of the citation sentence *outside* the final parenthesis.

## Checklist for Parentheticals

- If the case has less precedential value than the court's clear majority opinions, have you included a weight of authority parenthetical that follows the examples in Rule 10.6.2?
- If the relevance of the cited authority is not clear, have you included an explanatory parenthetical that follows the examples in B11 and Rules 10.6.1 and 10.6.2?
    - If so, have you used a present participle verb to begin your explanatory or commentary parenthetical? If you did not use a present participle verb, is the context of the explanation clear enough to warrant a shorter phrase?
- If you have both weight of authority and explanatory parentheticals, have you listed the weight of authority parenthetical first?
- If your citation includes prior or subsequent history, have you listed the parenthetical(s) immediately after the court and date parenthetical of the cited authority as shown in Rule 10.6.3?
- Have you left only one space before the opening parenthesis of the parenthetical?
- Have you put the period ending your citation sentence ***outside*** the final closing parenthesis?

## Exercise 13
## Parentheticals

Put the following information in correct *Bluebook* citation form. All sources are being cited in citation sentences. Assume that all citations will appear in a brief to a federal court. Although this exercise builds on the rules used in previous exercises, this exercise focuses on B5.1.4 and Rules 1.5, 1.6(d), 10.6.1, 10.6.2, and 12.7.

**Note:** In these problems, the wording for any explanatory phrase will appear in the text of the problem in quotation marks. Changes in wording will be read online as an error. This should not be construed as meaning that explanations have one "right" phrasing. This is simply a limitation imposed by having your work checked online.

**1.** Sandra Lockett, Petitioner, versus the State of Ohio, Respondent. This is a 1978 United States Supreme Court plurality opinion. It is reported in volume 438, page 586, of *United States Reports*; in volume 98, page 2954, of *Supreme Court Reporter*; and in volume 57, page 973, of *Lawyers' Edition*, Second Series.

______________________________________________

______________________________________________

______________________________________________

**2.** Williams, et al., versus Rhodes, Governor of Ohio, et al. This is a 1968 United States Supreme Court opinion. It is published in volume 393, page 23, of *United States Reports*, and in volume 45, page 236, of *Ohio Opinions*, Second Series. You wish to refer specifically to material appearing on page 37 of *United States Reports* in the concurring opinion of Justice Harlan.

______________________________________________

______________________________________________

______________________________________________

**3.** City of Chicago versus International College of Surgeons. This is a 1997 United States Supreme Court opinion. It is reported in volume 522, page 156, of *United States Reports*. You wish to cite from page 176 of Justice Ginsburg's dissenting opinion "suggesting that the majority used an improper standard of review."

______________________________________________

______________________________________________

______________________________________________

**4.** You wish to cite title 1, section 72, of West's *Maine Revised Statutes Annotated* "establishing 18 as the age of majority." This section appears entirely in the 1989 bound volume.

______________________________________________

______________________________________________

______________________________________________

5. Gary Newland versus Budget Rent-A-Car Systems, Incorporated. This is a February 2001 case from the Illinois Appellate Court, First District. It is reported in volume 744, page 902, of *North Eastern Reporter*, Second Series. You want to draw attention particularly to material on page 903 of the opinion "citing chapter 215, section 5/492.2 of the *Illinois Compiled Statutes*." This section appears in the 1998 main volume. [Note: You must properly draft the citation for section 5/492.2 to include in your parenthetical.]

____________________________________________________________

____________________________________________________________

____________________________________________________________

6. In the Matter of S.K. This is an October 13, 1989, per curiam opinion from the District of Columbia Court of Appeals (*not* the federal Circuit Court of Appeals for the District of Columbia). It is reported in volume 564, page 1382, of *Atlantic Reporter*, Second Series. You want to cite this case for its "holding that a civil proceeding predicated on abuse or neglect is remedial in nature."

____________________________________________________________

____________________________________________________________

____________________________________________________________

7. Exxon Corporation, Petitioner, versus Mary Tidwell and Terry Tidwell, Respondents. This is a 1993 case from the Texas Supreme Court. It is reported in volume 827, page 19, of *South Western Reporter*, Second Series. You want to explain to your reader that the court's holding was in the context of "remanding for a determination of whether the owner had direct control of the safety of the premises."

____________________________________________________________

____________________________________________________________

____________________________________________________________

8. You want to cite section 89, subsection (a), of title 14 of the current *United States Code*, published in 2000, "granting the Coast Guard authority to search and seize any vessel on the high seas subject to United States jurisdiction."

____________________________________________________________

____________________________________________________________

____________________________________________________________

9. In re Holliday's Tax Service, Incorporated. This is a 1976 federal district court case from the Eastern District of New York. It is reported in volume 417, page 182, of *Federal Supplement*. You want to cite the portion of the opinion on page 185 "holding that a corporation may appear in bankruptcy through its owner rather than an attorney." The Second Circuit Court of Appeals affirmed this decision in a 1976 opinion published in volume 614, page 1287, of *Federal Reporter*, Second Series.

____________________________________________________________

____________________________________________________________

____________________________________________________________

**10.** "Painting With Print: Incorporating Concepts of Typographic and Layout Design Into the Text of Legal Writing Documents," an article by Ruth Anne Robbins published in Fall 2004 in volume 2 of the Journal of the Association of Legal Writing Directors. This article "stating that well-used visual effects contribute to the emotional appeal of documents" appears on page 108.

______________________________________________

______________________________________________

______________________________________________

# Chapter 14

# SIGNALS

In the previous chapter, you learned that you can add parenthetical explanations to give your reader helpful information without making that information part of the text of your document. Citation signals are another tool you can use to give valuable information without a detailed explanation. Before reading the rest of this chapter, read all of B4 (including B4.1 through B4.5) and Rule 1.2 so you will be familiar with the type and identity of the signals available to you. Reading through the explanations of the signals first will provide a context for the following discussion.

You have probably noticed citation signals in citations in the legal reading you have done already. Signals can properly be used with any kind of cited authority. The purpose of signals is to show the reader how the authority cited relates to the text it follows and, in some cases, how it relates to other material in the same citation sentence. The eleven signals are divided into four categories of relationship: support, comparison, contradiction, and background.

| Support | Comparison | Contradiction | Background |
|---|---|---|---|
| [no signal] | *Compare* . . . | *Contra* | *See generally* |
| *E.g.,* | [and] . . . | *But see* | |
| *Accord* | *with* . . . | *But cf.* | |
| *See* | [and] . . . | | |
| *See also* | | | |
| *Cf.* | | | |

When you use a signal to describe the relationship between text and citation, a parenthetical explanation can be helpful in elaborating on that relationship. In fact, some relationships will not be clear to the reader without a parenthetical explanation. For that reason, *The Bluebook* often encourages or recommends the use of parentheticals with signals.

| No parentheticals | Parentheticals encouraged | Parentheticals strongly recommended |
|---|---|---|
| [no signal] | *See also* | *Cf.* |
| *E.g.,* | *See generally* | *Compare . . . with . . .* |
| *See* | | *But cf.* |
| *Accord* | | |
| *Contra* | | |
| *But see* | | |

Because the primary purpose of signals is to give the reader information without a detailed textual discussion, writers often take full advantage of signals by using one signal to introduce more than one source. When signals introduce more than one source, the sources are separated by semi-colons and ordered according to Rules 1.3 and 1.4. Rule 1.4 tells us how to order different types of authority in a single citation sentence (*e.g.*, cases and statutes) and also how to order authority of only one type in a single citation sentence (*e.g.*, cases from several jurisdictions). For example, if a citation sentence includes both a case and a journal article, Rule

1.4 instructs that the case (Rule 1.4(d)) should be listed before the article (Rule 1.4(i)).

> *Contra City of Los Angeles v. Lyons*, **461 U.S. 95** (1983); Brandon Garrett, Note, *Standing While Black: Distinguishing Lyons in Racial Profiling Cases*, **100 Colum. L. Rev. 1815** (2000).

On the other hand, if a citation sentence includes only cases, Rule 1.4(d) gives the order of cases within the sentences and also says that cases decided by the same court should be listed in reverse chronological order.

> *See, e.g., Heath v. Jones*, 817 S.W.2d 335 (**Tex. 1991**); *Cooper v. Smith*, 527 S.W.2d 898 (**Tex. 1975**); *Ludwick v. Miller*, 931 S.W.2d 752 (**Tex. App.—Fort Worth 1996**, no writ).

Writers can also maximize the use of signals by using more than one signal in a citation sentence. This is helpful when you want to describe both the relationship of the citations to the text and the relationship of the citations to one another. Rule 1.3 gives three rules for ordering signals:

- Signals should appear in the order listed in Rule 1.2.

> ***Accord*** *State v. Michaels*, 642 A.2d 1372 (N.J. 1994); ***see also*** *Commonwealth v. Allen*, 665 N.E.2d 105, 108-09 (Mass. App. Ct. 1996).

- Signals of the same type (*e.g.*, support) must appear in a single citation sentence separated by semi-colons (see above example).
- Signals of different types must be in separate citation sentences (see example in Rule 1.3).

As with all other parts of a legal citation, signals have specific typeface rules. Introductory signals in citations are always italicized in court documents and legal memoranda, as provided in B13 (page 24). Signals are punctuated according to the list in Rule 1.2. Notice that commas are only used with *e.g.* Notice also that the comma following *e.g.* is not italicized, while a comma within a signal is italicized along with other words in the signal (*See, e.g.,*). This is consistent with a rule you are already familiar with, Rule 2.1(f), which requires that commas within a case name be italicized while the comma following a case name is not. Remember, too, that a citation sentence has the same capitalization rules as a textual sentence: The first word must be capitalized. Therefore, a signal that begins a citation sentence is capitalized; otherwise, the signal is not capitalized.

> ***Accord*** *State v. Michaels*, 642 A.2d 1372 (N.J. 1994); ***see also*** *Commonwealth v. Allen*, 665 N.E.2d 105, 108-09 (Mass. App. Ct. 1996).

Before you begin the exercise, let's go through an example of a citation that uses a signal and a parenthetical.

Suppose we want to cite *Rancher v. Farmer*, 888 P.2d 222 (Mont. 1985), because it is additional source material to the more recent cases we have been discussing in text. *Rancher v. Farmer*, as well as the cases we have discussed, clearly supports the argument we have made. The point for which we are citing the case is that the court held that X is not Y in Montana. The question is, how can we indicate all that without having actually to discuss the case in text? Easy: Introductory signals to the rescue!

First, look at Rule 1.2, the signal rule. Quickly scanning subsection (a) we see that the first four signals listed do not quite describe our situation, but the fifth one, *see also*, looks good. *See also* best describes the relationship between this citation and the text, because we have already discussed several cases that support the textual proposition. We wish to use *Rancher v. Farmer* only as additional source material.

*See also Rancher v. Farmer*, 888 P.2d 222 (Mont. 1985)

Notice that no comma follows the signal.

Reading further in the description of *see also* in Rule 1.2, we find that the use of a parenthetical explanation with *see also* is encouraged to help the reader understand the relevance of the cited material. How will we write our parenthetical? Remember from the previous chapter and Rule 1.5 that an explanatory parenthetical phrase should begin with a present participle verb, so consider the various *-ing* verbs that spring to mind. Here, what the court *held* is exactly our point and explains the relevance of *Rancher v. Farmer* in the context of our argument. All we have to do, then, is change "held" to "holding" and proceed with the rest of the phrase. So our finished parenthetical will be as follows:

(holding that X is not Y).

Remember from Rule 10.6.3 that the explanatory parenthetical will follow the court and date element of the basic citation. Our final citation, complete with signal and parenthetical, then, will look like this:

*See also Rancher v. Farmer*, 888 P.2d 222 (Mont. 1985) (holding that X is not Y).

Remember to put a single space between the court and date parenthetical and the explanatory parenthetical. Also remember that the period at the end of the citation sentence goes outside the parentheses.

And that's all there is to it!

## Checklist for Signals

- Does your authority directly state the proposition, identify the source of a quotation, or identify an authority you mentioned in text?
    - If so, you can skip the rest of this checklist because "[no signal]" fills the bill.
    - If not, you must have a signal, so continue.
- Have you selected the appropriate signal from Rule 1.2?
- Have you only included commas in the signal if the signal is or includes *e.g.*?
- Have you italicized the signal?
- If your signal requires commas, have you italicized only those commas that fall within the signal?
- Have you capitalized the signal if it is the first word of your citation sentence?
- Have you left out any commas that are not shown in the examples in Rule 1.2?
- Does the citation need an explanatory parenthetical?
    - If not, you can skip the rest of the items in this checklist because the items following this one deal exclusively with parentheticals.
    - If so, continue through the checklist.
- Have you drafted a brief explanation describing the relevance of the citation?
- Have you selected an appropriate verb to begin your parenthetical explanation?
- Have you put that appropriate verb into *-ing* form?
- Have you put the period that ends the citation sentence outside the final parenthesis?

## Exercise 14
## Signals

Put the following information in correct *Bluebook* citation form. All sources are being cited in citation sentences. Although this exercise builds on the rules used in the previous exercises, this exercise focuses on B4 and Rules 1.2, 1.3, and 1.4. Determine what, if any, introductory signal you should use and what, if any, parenthetical explanation you should include.

**Note:** Where a rule relating to a signal encourages or recommends a parenthetical explanation, the correct answer on the *ICW* will include one. Likewise, where the signal rule does not call for an explanatory parenthetical phrase, the correct answer will not include one. As in the Parentheticals exercise, the wording for any needed parenthetical phrase will appear in quotation marks.

1. In a brief to the United States District Court for the Northern District of Texas, you quote directly from Wonder Labs, Incorporated, Plaintiff, versus Procter & Gamble Company, Defendant. This is a 1990 case from the United States District Court for the Southern District of New York. It is reported in volume 728, page 1058, of *Federal Supplement.* The material you quoted appears on page 1061. Draft the citation that should follow the quote.

2. In a trial brief arguing the validity of a covenant-not-to-compete clause of an employment contract, you write that "courts restrict employees' rights in a number of ways." To provide authority and background for this statement, you want to cite an article by William Lynch Schaller "discussing the evolution of restrictions on employee mobility." The Summer 2001 article is titled "Jumping Ship: Legal Issues Relating to Employee Mobility in High Technology Industries" and is published in volume 17, page 25, of the non-consecutively-paginated Labor Lawyer. Draft the citation that should follow your statement.

3. In a brief to the United States District Court, District of Colorado, you write that "political candidates are expected to represent not only their own views but also those of their political party." You inferred this expectation from a statement in Federal Election Commission, Plaintiff, versus Colorado Republican Federal Campaign Committee, Defendant. This is a February 18, 1999, case from the District Court for the District of Colorado. It is reported in volume 41, page 1197, of *Federal Supplement*, Second Series. Draft the citation that should follow your statement.

4. In a trial brief in a copyright infringement action, you write that "a number of courts have held that the First Amendment does not mandate acceptance of the parody defense." This proposition can be inferred from many opinions in which courts rejected the defendants' arguments that the First Amendment required acceptance of the parody defense. However, citation to a couple of those opinions will be sufficient to make your point. You have first chosen a Ninth Circuit Court of Appeals case to illustrate the point. That opinion is Sid & Marty Krofft Television Productions, Incorporated, versus McDonald's Corporation and Needham, Harper & Steers, Inc. This is a 1977 case reported in volume 562, page 1157, of *Federal Reporter*, Second Series.

   The second case you have chosen to illustrate your point is a 1981 case from the United States District Court, Southern District of New York styled Groucho Marx Productions, Incorporated, and Susan Marx, as Trustee under the Last Will and Testament of Harpo Marx, Plaintiffs, versus Day and Night Company, Incorporated, Alexander Cohen and the Shubert Organization, Defendants. It is reported in volume 523, page 485, of *Federal Supplement*. Draft the citation that should follow your statement.

______________________________________________

______________________________________________

______________________________________________

5. You write that "the governmental immunity provision requiring notice prior to filing suit applies to minors just as it does to adults." Although your research did not find a case directly on point for this proposition, you did find a case "holding that an action filed under the Liquor Control Act was barred, even to minors, by failing to give notice." This case is Beatrice Lowrey, et al., Appellants, versus Edward Malkowski, et al., Appellees. This is a 1960 case from the Supreme Court of Illinois. It is reported in volume 170, page 147, of *North Eastern Reporter*, Second Series. Although the holding in *Lowrey* is different from the proposition in your brief, it is sufficiently analogous to lend support to your position. Draft the citation that should follow your statement.

______________________________________________

______________________________________________

______________________________________________

6. In a motion to dismiss filed in the First Circuit, you write that "federal circuits are split on the issue of whether a federal cause of action for interspousal wiretapping should be recognized." You wish to offer support for this proposition by comparing a case from a jurisdiction that does recognize the cause of action with one that does not. The first case is Elizabeth Graham Flowers and Frankie Dukes, Appellees, versus Tandy Corporation and William Lee Flowers, Appellants. Flowers is a 1985 Fourth Circuit case "holding that a cause of action does not exist." It is reported in volume 773, page 585, of *Federal Reporter*, Second Series. The second case is Anonymous, Plaintiff-Appellant, versus Anonymous, Defendant-Appellee. Anonymous is a 1977 Second Circuit case "holding that a cause of action does exist." It is reported in volume 558, page 677, of *Federal Reporter*, Second Series. Draft the citation that should follow your statement. [Note: Remember to order authorities using Rule 1.4]

____________________________________________

____________________________________________

____________________________________________

7. In a brief to the Utah Supreme Court, you write that "bequests of money are not permitted in a memorandum." This rules comes directly from section 75-2-503 of the *Utah Code Annotated*, published in 1998. Draft the citation that should follow your statement.

____________________________________________

____________________________________________

____________________________________________

8. In a brief to the New Hampshire Supreme Court, you argue that your client, the testator of a contested will, was present when his will was witnessed. You believe that the testator did not have to look directly at the witnesses as they signed in order to be "present." In direct support of this proposition, you discuss a case from Illinois that closely mirrors the facts of your client's case. That case is an 1898 Illinois Supreme Court case styled Omer H. Drury versus James H. Connell and reported in volume 52, page 368, of *North Eastern Reporter*. Although no New Hampshire cases are directly on point, you wish to further support your argument with a New Hampshire case that is sufficiently similar to let the reader know that the Illinois law you have discussed in detail is consistent with the law of New Hampshire. The New Hampshire case you wish to cite is a 1904 Supreme Court of New Hampshire case styled Healey v. Bartlett and reported in volume 73, page 110, of *New Hampshire Reports* and in volume 59, page 617, of *Atlantic Reporter*. Draft the citation including both cases that should follow your argument. You may assume that the usual practice in New Hampshire is to cite both state and regional reporters.

____________________________________________

____________________________________________

____________________________________________

**9.** In a brief to the Massachusetts Appeals Court, you wish to cite Lorillard Tobacco Company, et al., versus Thomas F. Reilly, Attorney General of Massachusetts, et al. This 2001 United States Supreme Court case is not yet published in *United States Reports*. However, it is reported in volume 121, page 2404, of *Supreme Court Reporter*. You wish to indicate in your citation that this case is an additional source that supports the same proposition as the case you have discussed in the immediately preceding text. You also want to explain through your citation that the case is relevant because it cites chapter 93A, section 2, of the General Laws of the Commonwealth of Massachusetts (published in the 1997 main volume). Draft the citation that should follow your text.

______________________________________________

______________________________________________

______________________________________________

**10.** In an office memorandum written for general counsel of a hospital, you write that "children have historically been barred from participating in clinical trials, and that bar is likely to continue." You wish to let the attorney know that the contrary view (i.e. that children should be permitted to participate in clinical trials) is supported by a 2000 law review article in volume 28, page 362, of the Journal of Law, Medicine and Ethics. The article titled "The Ethics of Clinical Trials: A Child's View" was written by Jennifer Rosato. Draft the citation that should follow your statement.

______________________________________________

______________________________________________

______________________________________________

# Chapter 15
# LEGISLATIVE RESOURCES

Legislative history and administrative resources can be seen as the bookends bracketing volumes of statutes. Legislative history documents reflect and give insight into the process by which a particular bill either becomes or does not become enacted law. At the other end of the process, the regulatory agencies promulgate regulations that put the enacted statute into effect. The documents generated by regulatory agencies and by the rest of the executive branch of government are collectively referred to as administrative resources. Accordingly, rules governing use and citation of legislative resources begin in Chapter 12, which also covers enacted statutes. Chapter 13 focuses on additional legislative materials, and Chapter 14 contains provisions for citing administrative resources. For convenience, this chapter of the *ICW* is divided into two subsections: legislative history resources and administrative resources.

## A. Legislative History

This chapter and the accompanying exercises focus exclusively on federal materials. States vary widely in the publication of legislative materials, but many state legislative materials are patterned generally after the federal model. Therefore, the citation of legislative history follows the same general principles, whether federal or state.

In an increasingly codified legal system, statutory interpretation becomes a vital skill in many areas of legal practice. Often, a legal writer will rely on the intent of the legislature enacting a statute to properly interpret that statute. Legal writers look to the documents that are produced in the legislative process to determine that legislative intent.

To understand how to cite these documents, let's refamiliarize ourselves with the path a bill takes through Congress on its way to becoming "law." As we walk through that progression, we will take side excursions into sections of *The Bluebook* that show how to cite the publications at each step. Let's trace a wholly fictional bill from a Congressman's desk into the pages of the *United States Code*.

In the first session of the 104th Congress, Representative Blue introduces a bill he calls the Excellence in Legal Writing Act of 1999. This bill is the 911th bill introduced into the House of Representatives during this session, so the number given to the bill is H.R. 911. Rule 13.2(a) would govern citation of the **unenacted bill** at this point:

Excellence in Legal Writing Act, H.R. 911, 104th Cong. (1999).

Our bill is referred to the House Committee on Education, which in turn refers it to its subcommittee on Improvement of the Legal Profession, which then conducts hearings. The printed transcript of the hearing shows on its cover the title "Excellence in Legal Writing Act: Hearing on H.R. 911 Before the Subcommittee on Improvement of the Legal Profession of the House Committee on Education." According to Rule 13.3, we cite to committee hearings by including the title, which should include the bill number and the name of the subcommittee and committee, the number of the Congress, the page number, if any, and the year. If we cite to a particular part of the testimony at the hearings, we include a page number and a final parenthetical statement explaining whose testimony we are citing. B6.1.6 tells us to italicize the title, and we must abbreviate the words in the title according to T.6, T.10 and T.11.

*Excellence in Legal Writing Act: Hearings on H.R. 911 Before the Subcomm. on Improving the Legal Profession of the House Comm. on Educ.*, 104th Cong. 27–28 (1999) (statement of Mary Smith, law student).

After hearings, the committee votes to recommend passage of our bill. The committee submits the bill, as amended, in a committee report. Committee reports are good sources of legislative history, including changes to the language of the bill and an explanation of the reasons behind the committee's recommendation. Committee reports are numbered sequentially. A citation to a report, according to Rule 13.4(a), will include the name of the house, the number of the Congress and the number of the report, a page number, and a year of publication. B6.1.6 tells us that the citation should appear in plain roman type. If the House report on our bill is the 83rd report this session, a cite to page 5 of the report would look like this:

H.R. Rep. No. 104-83, at 5 (1999).

For some but not all bills, House and Senate reports, as well as recent conference reports, are reprinted, together with the related bill, in the *United States Code Congressional and Administrative News* (abbreviated U.S.C.C.A.N. and informally called "you–scan"). When a legislative resource is available in U.S.C.C.A.N., you should give a parallel cite to it, as provided in Rule 13.4(a).[1] Our committee report is one of the documents reprinted in the permanent 1999 edition of that publication beginning at page 6144:

H.R. Rep. No. 104–83, at 5 (1999), *reprinted in* 1999 U.S.C.C.A.N. 6144.

Now, back to our bill! Our bill now goes to the floor of the House for a vote. The bill is debated on the floor of the House, and the *Congressional Record* includes a transcript of the debate. The *Congressional Record* is published daily during each legislative session. At the end of each session, all daily editions are published in a permanent, bound edition. The rule governing citation to the debate is Rule 13.5. If the debate is published on page 23,251 of volume 143 of the permanent edition of the *Congressional Record*, our citation would look like this:

143 Cong. Rec. 23,251 (1999).

If we were citing the debate before the permanent edition of that volume of the *Congressional Record* became available, Rule 13.5 tells us that we would cite to the daily edition. That means that we would give the full date, remembering to abbreviate the month as shown in T.12, and that information would become part of the parenthetical. Notice that an "H" precedes the page number in the daily edition citation because the daily editions are separated into House and Senate proceedings, each with its own consecutive pagination. The page numbers in the separate volumes are preceded by either an "H" or an "S" so we will know which section of the daily edition, House or Senate, to consult:

143 Cong. Rec. H12,345 (daily ed. Apr. 14, 1999). [2]

---

[1] When citing to a report reprinted in U.S.C.C.A.N., *The Bluebook* gives two conflicting examples. In Rule 13.1, the U.S.C.C.A.N. information is added to a citation with the words "*reprinted in.*" In an example under Rule 13.5, the U.S.C.C.A.N. information follows the words "*as reprinted in.*" For purposes of consistency, the *ICW* will use the rule given in 13.1.

[2] On Lexis and Westlaw, all *Congressional Record* cite page numbers are preceded by "H" or "S" even after the document is printed in the permanent edition. However, your citations should follow the Bluebook rule of eliminating the "H" or "S" once it is published in the permanent edition.

Notice that in the two preceding citation examples, a comma appears in the page numbers. Rule 6.2(a) tells us that when a number has five digits or more, we must separate it into groups of three digits by comma.[3]

Our bill passes the House! After approval by the House of Representatives, the bill is sent to the Senate for consideration. The Senate will have similar committee hearings and debates on our bill. Once the Senate also passes it, it is assigned a session law number. Most federal session laws are called Public Laws, and Public Law numbers reflect simply the number of the Congress, here the 104th, and the chronological order of the enactment. The law we are tracing is the 205th law enacted by the 104th Congress; therefore, its session law number is Public Law 104–205, abbreviated "Pub. L." as shown in Rule 12.4. We also include the year of passage of the bill in a date parenthetical. The session law citation is as follows:

Excellence in Legal Writing Act, **Pub. L. No. 104–205** (1999).

Federal session laws are compiled in *United States Statutes at Large*, which, as T.1 indicates, is abbreviated "Stat." Our newly enacted statute appears on page 683 of volume 127 of *United States Statutes at Large*. When the statute appears in that source, its citation will include that information:

Excellence in Legal Writing Act, Pub. L. No. 104–205, **127 Stat. 683** (1999).

Notice that Rule 12.4(d) also tells us to omit the date parenthetical if the year is part of the name of the statute. If the year of enactment were part of the title of this statute, the citation would look like this:

Excellence in Legal Writing Act of 1999, Pub. L. No. 104–205, 127 Stat. 683.

When you know where the enacted statute will be codified (usually this information is part of the enacted bill itself), include that information parenthetically in its citation, as Rule 12.4(e) provides. Thus if our statute will be codified as section 1331 of title 53 of the *United States Code*, its citation will reflect this information:

Excellence in Legal Writing Act, Pub. L. No. 104–205, 127 Stat. 683 **(1999) (to be codified at 53 U.S.C. § 1331).**

Once the act is codified, you will ordinarily cite it as a statute according to the provisions of Chapter 12. However, occasionally you may have a specific reason to cite the bill or the session law. For example, you may wish to cite to the session law when it is codified in many scattered sections or titles of the official code, as provided in Rule 12.2(a). In addition, you would also want to cite to the original bill to show amendments and to document legislative history, as provided in 13.2(b).

Much of the time you will research and compile the legislative history of a statute that applies to your case yourself. Some particularly important federal acts, however, are the subjects of separately bound legislative histories. They would be cited according to the same rules as those governing citation of books and other nonperiodic materials, Rule 15 of *The Bluebook*. You will learn more about the sources of already compiled legislative histories in your research course. Among other valuable lessons, you will learn that if a legislative history has already been

---

[3] However, the Eighteenth Edition of *The Bluebook* deleted an example from Rule 6.2(a) that showed a comma being used with a daily edition page reference: "H17,326." Perhaps the legislative history of Rule 6.2(a) suggests that a comma should not be used with a daily edition page reference. Until this mystery is resolved, the *ICW* will follow the text of Rule 6.2(a) and require a comma.

compiled, you will save valuable research time if you use it rather than re-inventing that particular wheel.

**B. Administrative Resources**

Just as enacted statutes are positive law, so are the administrative rules and regulations that implement them. Administrative regulations originate with the agencies and departments of the executive branch of government. Take a couple of minutes now to scan the provisions of Rule 14 and familiarize yourself with its contents. You will see that, as in other areas of *The Bluebook*, the coverage is briefly described in Rule 14, and Rule 14.1 demonstrates the basic citation forms of administrative and executive materials. Rules 14.5 and 14.6 contain specialized provisions relating to federal tax and SEC (Securities and Exchange Commission) materials, areas outside the scope of this exercise.

The primary sources of federal administrative materials are the ***Code of Federal Regulations*** and the ***Federal Register***. Rule 14.2(a) governs final rules and regulations published in the C.F.R., and Rule 14.2(b) deals with proposed rules and regulations found in the daily editions of the *Federal Register*, as well as administrative notices of numerous kinds.

The C.F.R. is the official compilation of codified rules and regulations and is organized and cited much like the *United States Code*. Both are arranged topically into titles; however, the titles of the U.S.C. and the C.F.R. do not parallel one another. The citation forms are also quite similar. If a rule or regulation has a familiar name, then you should include the name. Just as the title number precedes the abbreviation U.S.C., so the title number of the regulation precedes the abbreviation C.F.R. And just as the section number of the statute follows the code abbreviation, so the regulation section or part number follows its code abbreviation. Also like statutory citations, a citation to a regulation needs a date. This date is the date on the relevant volume of the C.F.R., not the date of adoption of the rule or regulation.

statute: Employee Retirement Income Security Act of 1974, 29 U.S.C. § 1132 (2000).

regulation: Employee Retirement Income Security Act of 1974, 25 C.F.R. 2510.3-1 (2007).

Rule 14.2(a) tells us to cite final rules to the *Code of Federal Regulations* if possible, or to the *Federal Register* if not, indicating parenthetically where the new rule will be codified. (If all this sounds familiar to you, aren't you glad you learned the federal statutory citation material so well?) Each title of the *Code of Federal Regulations* is revised each year, but not all at the same time. The revisions are spread out over four quarterly publication dates, January, April, July, and October. The date of each volume of *Code of Federal Regulations* appears on the cover.

As you have learned (or soon will learn) in legal research, when an administrative agency proposes (or promulgates) a regulation, notice of that proposed regulation is published in the *Federal Register*. When a regulation is adopted in its final form, it will appear first in the *Federal Register* and then in the *Code of Federal Regulations*. The *Federal Register* contains administrative notices, proposed regulations, and other announcements. Rule 14.2(b) tells us to cite notices of a proposed regulation the same way we would cite a final regulation, except that we must add the date of proposal to the normal date parenthetical.

Plans Established or Maintained Under or Pursuant to Collective Bargaining Agreements Under Section 3(40)(A) of ERISA, 65 Fed. Reg. 64,482-01 (proposed October 27, 2000) (to be codified at 29 C.F.R. pt. 2510).

If you cite only a part of a rule, as with a pinpoint citation to any source you must indicate in the full citation not only the beginning page of the rule, but also the specific page on which the cited material appears. The following pinpoint citation to a final rule demonstrates this:

Grants to Combat Violent Crimes Against Women on Campuses, 64 Fed. Reg. 39,774, 39,777 (1999) (to be codified at 28 C.F.R. pt. 90).

Where the relevance for the pinpoint citation is not obvious to the reader, Rule 1.5 on parenthetical information recommends an explanatory parenthetical.

Grants to Combat Violent Crimes Against Women on Campuses, 64 Fed. Reg. 39,774, 39,777 (1999) (to be codified at 28 C.F.R. pt. 90) (responding to a comment that the regulation was "too heavily oriented toward directing victims to the criminal justice system").

When an agency schedules a public hearing or a meeting or makes a public announcement, the *Federal Register* publishes the official notice.

Open Meeting Notice, 64 Fed. Reg. 51,755 (1999).

Although most of the administrative materials you will have occasion to cite in law school and in your law practice will probably be of the regulatory type, presidential proclamations, and executive orders are also administrative materials, and we cite them according to Rule 14.7. Proclamations and executive orders that are currently in force are published in the C.F.R. If not in the C.F.R. you may cite to the *Federal Register*. Some presidential documents are also reprinted in the statutory codes. If the document has been reprinted in the statutory code, give a parallel cite to the *United States Code*; if the document does not appear in the *United States Code* but does appear in one of the unofficial codes, *United States Code Annotated* (U.S.C.A.) or *United States Code Service* (U.S.C.S.), then use the unofficial code for the parallel citation.

Exec. Order No. 12,781, 3 C.F.R. 373 (1992), *reprinted in* 3 U.S.C.A. § 301 app. at 878–79 (West 1997).

Remember to check T.1 for the proper citation form for the unofficial code you are using.

Notice that the citation above is to a *page* number in the *Code of Federal Regulations*, not a *section* number. Because Presidential documents are not rules, they have no section numbers. Rule 14.7(a) sends us back to 14.2(a), where we learn that "in certain circumstances" we are to cite to page numbers rather than section or part numbers in the *Code of Federal Regulations*. Presidential papers constitute "certain circumstances" for the purpose of Rule 14.2.

Short forms for regulatory citations are discussed in Rule 14.10, which closely parallels the statutory short forms set forth in Rule 12.9. For example, if you had already given a full citation for the following final rule:

Regulations Governing Off-the-Record Communications, 18 C.F.R. § 385 (2007).

then as Rule 14.9(c) and B6.2 provide, a later citation to the same section after intervening cites would take the following form:

18 C.F.R. § 385.

or

§ 385.

See how easy it all is? Take it away, citation wizards!

# Exercise 15
# Legislative Resources

## A. Legislative History

Put the following information in correct *Bluebook* citation form. All sources are being cited in citation sentences in a brief to be filed in a federal court of appeals. Although this exercise builds on the rules used in the previous exercises, this exercise focuses on Rules 13–13.6, 12.2.2, and 12.4–12.7, and B13.

1. You want to cite to some background information given on page 5 of a committee report from the Committee of Energy and Commerce on the House of Representatives. This report, number 107-6, accompanies House bill number 724. The bill and the committee report have the same title, the Strategic Petroleum Reserve Reauthorization Act. The bill was introduced in the House on February 26, 2001, and the committee report was dated March 6, 2001. This report was not reprinted in U.S.C.C.A.N.

   ______________________________________________

   ______________________________________________

   ______________________________________________

2. In a discussion on the legislative history of certain laws passed following the attacks on the World Trade Center and the Pentagon on September 11, 2001, you wish to cite a session law called the Uniting and Strengthening America by Providing Appropriate Tools Required to Intercept and Obstruct Terrorism (USA Patriot Act) Act of 2001, published in volume 115 of the *United States Statutes at Large* at page 272. The bill was the 56th bill passed by both houses of Congress in October of 2001 during the 107th Congress. This act is known as the "USA Patriot Act."

   ______________________________________________

   ______________________________________________

   ______________________________________________

3. You are writing a memo to a supervising attorney on the status of a bill pending in Congress. You want to cite to the unenacted bill. The bill originated in the House of Representatives during the 107th Congress and was the 503rd bill introduced that session. Rep. Lindsey Graham introduced the bill on February 7, 2001.

   ______________________________________________

   ______________________________________________

   ______________________________________________

4. You wish to cite to a May 15, 2001 committee report on H.R. 73 (H. Con. Res. 73). The report was given a House report number of 107-40. The report was not published in U.S.C.C.A.N.

   ______________________________________________

   ______________________________________________

   ______________________________________________

5. You wish to cite to a statement of Rep. Louise Slaughter that was an extension of remarks made during a debate on the floor of the House of Representatives on Tuesday April 24, 2001. The entire testimony is available only in the daily edition of the *Congressional Record*, volume 147, pages E612 through E613.

6. You wish to cite a statement of Sen. Russell Feingold that was made on the floor of the Senate on July 10, 2001, on the death penalty. The transcript of this debate is found in the permanent edition of the *Congressional Record*, volume 147, page 7418.

7. You wish to cite to a joint resolution that has the House number 22. The resolution was introduced on February 27, 2001 in the 107th Congress and proposed a constitutional amendment prohibiting presidential pardons in the last three months of a presidential election year.

8. You want to quote some testimony from a committee hearing. The title on the cover is "A Review of H.R. 2413 — The Computer Security Enhancement Act of 1999," and the hearing was before the Technology Subcommittee of the House Committee on Science. The language you are quoting comes from page 2, a statement of Connie Morella, Chairwoman of the Technology Subcommittee. This hearing took place on September 30, 1999, during the 106th Congress.

9. In a discussion of the legislative history of the Video Privacy Protection Act of 1988, you cite to a 1988 report from the Senate Judiciary Committee. This report was the 599th report in the 100th Congress. You want to cite to information in part III(A) of the report.

## B. Administrative Resources

Put the following information in correct *Bluebook* citation form. All sources are being cited in citation sentences in a brief to be filed in a federal court of appeals. While this exercise builds on the rules used in previous exercises, this exercise focuses on Rules 14–14.4 and 14.7.

**1.** You are writing on wage and hour laws for minors, and you want to cite to new regulations promulgated by the Department of Labor. These regulations are found in title 29 of the *Code of Federal Regulations*, section 570.35. The last publication of this section was in 2008.

______________________________________________

______________________________________________

______________________________________________

**2.** Section 52.1531 of title 7 of the 2008 *Code of Federal Regulations* sets out the Department of Agriculture's standards for olive oil in the United States. You would like to cite this section.

______________________________________________

______________________________________________

______________________________________________

**3.** You need to cite to a proposed rule that would be codified in title 14 of the C.F.R., part 91. The rule was proposed on November 16, 2000, in volume 65 of the *Federal Register*, page 69,426.

______________________________________________

______________________________________________

______________________________________________

**4.** You need to cite to a final rule that will be codified in title 10 of the C.F.R., part 1040, regarding the implementation of Title IX. The rule appeared on January 18, 2008, in volume 66 of the *Federal Register*, page 4627.

______________________________________________

______________________________________________

______________________________________________

**5.** Draft a citation for Executive Order No. 13,223, signed on September 14, 2001, by President George W. Bush. This order is found in volume 66 of the *Federal Register*, page 48,201.

______________________________________________

______________________________________________

______________________________________________

**6.** Draft a citation for Presidential Proclamation No. 7463, signed on September 14, 2001, by President George W. Bush. This proclamation is found in volume 66 of the *Federal Register*, page 48,199.

______________________________________________

______________________________________________

______________________________________________

# Chapter 16
# ELECTRONIC, INTERNET & NONPRINT SOURCES

We have discussed how to cite to most print sources: cases we find in reporters, statutes we find in compilations, legislative history documents found in various government publications, and even common books, magazines and newspapers. However, each year the legal profession moves away from researching dusty volumes in corners of law libraries to "paperless" research. Many (if not most) cases, statutes, legislative history documents, and secondary sources are also available through electronic databases or on the Internet. Not only have commercial electronic databases such as Westlaw and LexisNexis become standard tools of the trade at many, if not most, law firms, but also Internet websites hosted by governmental or commercial entities have become numerous and easy to use. Rule 18 walks us through the proper citation forms for the various alternative sources to primary and secondary legal materials. In addition, Rule 18 contains citation forms for resources that were never in print but have become very accessible to the public: films, television broadcasts, videotapes, and audio recordings.

*The Bluebook* continues to prefer that legal writers cite to traditional printed sources for reasons of broad accessibility, authoritativeness, and permanence. However, *The Bluebook* does recognize that sometimes sources will only be found in nonprint sources or will be much easier to access using a nonprint source. Because our ultimate goal is to enable our reader to easily access the source using the information in our citation, Rule 18.1 strongly suggests that materials be cited to a well-known commercial database such as LexisNexis or Westlaw, even if the source is available over the Internet. Note that you use the citation format given in Rule 18.1 for these commercial providers regardless of whether you accessed their databases using a software package and a modem or using their Internet websites.

## A. Electronic Databases

### 1. Cases

If a case is not published in a reporter, then you should cite to a widely used electronic database that does contain that case. You should include the following information:

- the case name,
- the docket number,
- the database identifier and number of the case, if any,
- the court name, and
- the full date of the court decision.

*Case Name,* Docket Number, Database Name/Number (Court Month Day, Year).

*Washington v. Werner,* No. 96–8–00197–6, 1998 WL 283537 (Wash. Ct. App. June 2, 1998).

If you wish to use a pinpoint citation to focus your reader's attention on a particular page, remember that the pages given in the reporter are not as useful on a computer screen. Commercial databases assign pages in a process called "star pagination." A pinpoint to one of these pages would contain the word "at" and then an asterisk and the page number, even in the long form of the citation.

*Case Name*, Docket Number, Database Name/Number, **at *Pg** (Court Month Day, Year).

*Washington v. Werner*, No. 96–8–00197–6, 1998 WL 283537, at *2 (Wash. Ct. App. June 2, 1998).

The unique database identifier is retained in constructing a short form to a case found on an electronic database.

*Werner*, 1998 WL 283537, at *2.

### 2. Statutes

A cite to a statute or constitutional provision that you have found on an electronic database is identical to a citation to the printed code except in the date parenthetical. Remember, the date in the parenthetical is the publication date of the volume of the code, not the date of adoption of the statute. In an electronic database, statutes are updated on a rolling basis without set publication dates of volumes and pocket parts. However, electronic databases do tell you how current the statute is that you are reading on your computer screen with language such as "current through the 2008 legislative session." You add this information, plus any commercial publisher's name, and the name of the database in the date parenthetical.

Wash. Rev. Code Ann. § 9.41.280(1)(a) (West, WESTLAW through 2007 Spec. Sess.).

Because statutes are not assigned a unique database identifier, the short form for a statute found on an electronic database will look eerily similar to a short form for a statute found in a bound volume.

§ 9.41.280(1)(a).

### 3. Legislative, Administrative, and Executive Materials

Similarly, legislative, administrative, and executive materials accessed through an electronic database are cited identically to their print counterparts, except that the name of the database and any assigned numbers are added at the end of the citation. The concept is similar to parallel citation.

H.R. Rep. No. 104–83, at 5 (1999), *reprinted in* 1999 U.S.C.C.A.N. 6144, 1995 WL 217371 (Leg. Hist.)

### 4. Secondary Materials

Probably the most convenient feature of electronic databases is the easy searching of secondary sources. When you access these sources through an electronic database, cite as you would to the printed resource, with a "parallel" cite to the database and identifier.

Stephen R. Heifetz, *Blue in the Face: The Bluebook, the Bar Exam, and the Paradox of Our Legal Culture*, 51 Rutgers L. Rev. 695 (1999), *available at* 51 RULR 695.

## B. Internet Sources

Although *The Bluebook* expresses reservations about the permanence and authoritativeness of sites on the World Wide Web, Rule 18.2 does allow for citation to sources accessed or accessible via the Internet when either the source is not available in print or on an electronic database or the citation to the Internet resource will materially increase accessibility to the reader. If the source is available both in a traditional medium and online, then the Internet information, including the Uniform Resource Locator (URL), is treated like a type of parallel cite. *The Bluebook* does encourage authors to maintain print or download copies of Internet sources because of these sources' transient nature. However, the cite need not note the archival with information like "last visited" or "on file with the author."

Rule 18.2.2 states that if a case is accessible through a traditional source, but you would like to include Internet information as an aid to your reader, then you append the Internet information to the basic case citation after the court and date parenthetical.

*Case Name,* Vol. Reporter Pg. (Court Date), *available at* URL.

*United States v. Bajakajian,* 524 U.S. 321 (1998), *available at* http://supct.law.cornell.edu/supct/cases/name.htm.

If a case is only available via the Internet, then Rule 18.2.3 tells you to include the Internet information in the following manner:

*Case Name,* Docket No. (Court Month Date, Year), URL.

*San Antonio Area Found. v. Lang* No. 99-14-1117 (Tex. Nov. 9, 2000), http://www.supreme.courts.state.tx.us/opinions991117o.htm.

A short form to an Internet case cite according to Rule 18.7(c) should follow the rules appropriate for a case short form, with the URL added.

*Bajakajian,* 524 U.S. at 323, *available at* http://supct.law.cornell.edu/supct/cases/name.htm.

Rule 18.2.2 applies to all sources covered by *Bluebook* Rules 10–17. Therefore, a parallel citation to an electronic source can be given to any type of authority you've learned to cite.

I.R.C. § 401, *available at* http://www.access.gpo.gov/congress/cong013.html

H.R. Rep. No. 104-83, at 5 (1999), *reprinted in* 1999 U.S.C.C.A.N. 6144, *available at* http://thomas.loc.gov.

Employee Retirement Income Security Act of 1974, 29 C.F.R. § 2510.3-1 (1999), *available at* http://www.dol.gov/dol/allcfr/Title_29/Part_2510/29CFR2510.3-1.htm.

Linda Greenhouse, *Supreme Court Bars Traffic Roadblocks Intended to Check for Drugs,* N.Y. Times, Nov. 29, 2000, at A1, *available at* www.ny-t.com.

Increasingly, the Internet is becoming a place of original publication, not just a place to duplicate content that appeared first in print. Rule 18.2.3 tells you how to cite original web content. Because your first year course will likely not focus on this type of source, this chapter will not treat those sources in detail.

From time to time you may also need to cite to a nonprint source such as a video recording or an audio recording. The rules for these types of infrequent citations appear in Rules 18.5 and 18.6.

Although Rule 18 casts a wide net to cover many types of nontraditional sources, the basic rules for each type of source are similar. With *The Bluebook* in hand, you should be able to cite to any source found in an electronic database or on the Internet with ease!

## Exercise 16
## Electronic, Internet & Nonprint Sources

Put the following information in correct *Bluebook* citation form. All sources are being cited in citation sentences. Although this exercise builds on the rules used in the previous exercises, this exercise focuses on Rule 18. You should follow the convention of placing one space after a colon, period, or question mark within a title.

1. Boulware v. United States. This is a March 3, 2008, case from the United States Supreme Court. The docket number for this case is 06-1509. The case is not yet published in a reporter. However, this case is available on the U.S. Supreme Court's web site at http://www.supremecourtus.gov/opinions/07pdf/06-1509.pdf. You wish to cite this slip opinion at page 2.

___

___

___

2. "Why Pakistan Matters" an article by Simon Robinson, published in the January 14, 2008, issue of Time. The article appears on page 42. The article is accessible online at http://www.time.com/time/world/article/0,8599,1699642,00.html.

___

___

___

3. "Sexualized Advocacy: The Ascendant Backlash Against Female Lawyers," an article by Kathleen A. Bergin, published in 2006 in volume 18 of the Yale Journal of Law & Feminism. The article appears on page 191 of this consecutively paginated journal. The article is also available in Westlaw with the unique database identifier of 18 YJLF 191.

___

___

___

4. House of Representatives Report 107-125, released on July 10, 2001, by the Committee on the Judiciary. The report does not appear in U.S.C.C.A.N. This report is accessible at http://thomas.loc.gov/cp107/cp107query.html.

___

___

___

5. You want to cite to a statement of Senator Barak Obama that was made on the floor of the Senate on April 26, 2007. The transcript of this debate is found in the permanent edition of the *Congressional Record*, volume 153, page 5177. The report is also available at http://thomas.loc.gov/home/r110query.html.

___

___

___

6. You are researching Texas family law for an office memorandum. Your law office does not have any state materials, but you found the applicable provision, Tex. Fam. Code Ann. § 8.001, using LexisNexis. The screen in LexisNexis states that the text as it appears is current through the end of the 2007 Regular Session.

_______________________________________________

_______________________________________________

_______________________________________________

7. In doing some research for a brief, you find a case from the Arkansas Supreme Court, styled Larry Wayne Goodnight, Appellant, versus State of Arkansas, Appellee. This case was decided on January 10, 2008. This case is unreported, but you found it at http://courts.arkansas.gov/unpublished/2008a/20080110/cr07-746.pdf

_______________________________________________

_______________________________________________

_______________________________________________

8. "Fostering Respect for Our Students, Our Specialty, and Our Legal Profession: Introducing Ethics and Professionalism Into the Legal Writing Curriculum,' an article by Melissa H. Weresh, published in 2006 in volume 21, page 427, of the Touro Law Review. You found this article in LexisNexis with the unique database identifier, 21 Touro L. Rev. 427.

_______________________________________________

_______________________________________________

_______________________________________________

9. In re Wollheim. This is a February 14, 2008, case from the Supreme Court of Oregon. At this time, the case is not yet published in a reporter. However, it is available on Westlaw. The unique database identifier is 2008 WL 384248. The docket number is 06-87. [Note: A case that has not yet been published is not the same as an opinion that has been designated "unpublished" by the court.]

_______________________________________________

_______________________________________________

_______________________________________________

# Chapter 17
# WHEN DO I CITE?

We have often found that in teaching our students the intricacies of legal citation rules, we need to stop and focus on the most important citation rule: The rule that tells us when we must cite! Knowing when to cite can be tricky until you have some experience in writing legal memoranda, court documents, or a scholarly paper. You probably have brought some citation placement experience with you from your undergraduate or graduate work. For better or worse, legal writing requires very precise and usually frequent citation of the propositions in our legal writing — probably more precision and frequency than writing in other fields.

The general rule of thumb for legal memoranda and court documents is that you need a citation for every fact, thought, or opinion that comes from another source (not you or your facts). You need a citation even if you are not quoting. The purpose of your citation is to enable your reader to go to a specific page of a specific source and find support for the sentence preceding the citation. If you are detailing the facts of a case or the holding of a case, then you need a citation to that case, whether you are quoting or paraphrasing. If you are quoting or paraphrasing a statute or regulation, then you need a citation. If you are making a proposition about the state of the law generally, then you need a citation to a source that supports that proposition. If you are providing your reader with a rule that you have synthesized from several sources, then you need cites to those sources. Here are some examples of the types of sentences you will write in a legal memorandum or a court document that would need citations:

> In our jurisdiction, courts look to numerous factors when determining whether an individual can establish ownership by adverse possession. *Belotti v. Bickhardt,* 127 N.E. 239 (N.Y. 1920).
>
> The Court of Appeals of New York held that the defendant's possession must be hostile and under a claim of right; the possession must be actual; the possession must be "open and notorious"; the possession must be exclusive; and the possession must be continuous for a period of twenty years. *Belotti v. Bickhardt,* 127 N.E. 239, 241 (N.Y. 1920).
>
> The defendant used and rented all portions of a building, a portion of which was built on property owned by the plaintiff. *Belotti v. Bickhardt,* 127 N.E. 239, 240 (N.Y. 1920).

However, you do not need a citation when detailing your own facts or even applying a previously cited rule to your facts. If in doubt, ask yourself: "If my reader turns to this page of this source, would the reader find support for this statement?" Here are some examples to illustrate:

> Tina Trespasser, our client, should be able to show that she meets all five of the requirements to prove adverse possession.
>
> Tina, like the defendant in *Belotti,* has continuously occupied the land in question and earned income from it.

Notice that some of the examples in this chapter cite to the first page of the case only, while others pinpoint the location of specific material cited. When authority is used to represent a rule of law (*e.g.*, a landmark decision like *Roe v. Wade* for the right to privacy), then the citation does not necessarily require a pinpoint. However, when your citation follows facts or reasoning from the case, a pinpoint citation is needed to help your reader find the information cited.

Now that you know how to cite and when to cite, you're all set!

## Exercise 17
## When Do I Cite?

For this exercise, you will use a set of facts about a fictitious client and two actual cases. You will be given sentences taken in order from a hypothetical discussion section in a legal memorandum. You will need to decide whether each sentence requires a citation to one of the given cases. If you determine that the sentence does not require a citation, then simply leave the space after the sentence blank. (If you are doing this exercise on the website, type "no citation" in plain type in the solution box and click "submit.") If you determine that the sentence does require a citation, then simply type either "Exxon" or "Gonzalez" in plain type, as applicable. All citations will be citations sentences. Remember to use the full citation form, "*id.*," or an abbreviated short form when necessary.

Facts: Your client is Kendall Loeb. Mr. Loeb lives across the street from a convenience store, The Quik Shop. On August 7, 2001, in the parking lot of the store, Mr. Loeb had an argument with another customer. The customer threatened to kill him and then sped out of the parking lot. Mr. Loeb asked the store attendant, who heard the threat, to call the police, and the attendant refused. As Mr. Loeb was walking back to his house, the customer returned in his truck and hit Mr. Loeb with the truck. Mr. Loeb has filed suit against the store for negligently failing to protect him from the other customer's assault.

Cases: *Exxon Corp. v. Tidwell*, 867 S.W.2d 19 (Tex. 1993). This is the most recent Texas Supreme Court opinion that states the general rule that a landowner has no duty to protect invitees on the premises from criminal acts of third parties. An exception to this rule occurs when the owner both has direct control of the safety and security of the premises and could have foreseen the criminal acts. This case does not focus on the "foreseeability" exception. The rule and exceptions are stated on page 20 of the court's opinion

*Gonzalez v. S. Dallas Club*, 951 S.W.2d 72 (Tex. 1992). This case focuses on the "foreseeability" exception. The court specifies the circumstances in which a criminal act would be foreseeable. The court's holding and rationale are on page 76. The facts appear on page 73.

1. In Texas, the plaintiff in a successful cause of action for negligent failure to protect must demonstrate that a store owner or his agent (1) had direct control over the safety and security of the premises, and (2) could have foreseen the criminal act that resulted in the plaintiff's injury.

_______________________________________________

_______________________________________________

_______________________________________________

2. In our case, the parties do not dispute that the owner of The Quik Shop and his agents had direct control over the safety and security of the premises. However, the parties do disagree about whether the criminal acts were foreseeable.

_______________________________________________

_______________________________________________

_______________________________________________

3. To prove that a criminal act is foreseeable, we will have to show that the owner or his agent knew or should have known that assault was the type of crime that routinely occurred in that area or that the specific confrontation would result in criminal assault once the parties left the premises.

4. The owner of The Quik Shop clearly should have foreseen that a confrontation beginning on the premises would result in a criminal act off the premises.

5. In Texas, an owner who operates a business in a high-crime area can foresee that criminal acts may occur on the premises. Additionally, an owner can foresee that a confrontation on the premises may lead to a criminal act off the premises when one customer threatens another before leaving the premises.

6. In *Gonzalez v. S. Dallas Club*, the Court of Appeals held that an owner could not have foreseen a later injury to a patron when the manager escorted the patron through the back door of the club following a confrontation and watched her drive away.

7. The court held that an owner cannot foresee a later criminal act when he takes all necessary steps to provide for the safety of a customer by making sure that the customer leaves the premises safely.

8. The events of August 7 are very different from the events discussed in *Gonzalez*.

9. Although the store attendant knew that Mr. Loeb had been threatened, he made no attempt to help Mr. Loeb leave the premises safely as the manager in *Gonzalez* had done.

**10.** In addition, the attendant did not call the police to protect Mr. Loeb even though Mr. Loeb specifically asked him to.

______________________________________________

______________________________________________

______________________________________________

# Chapter 18
# COURT DOCUMENTS

So far, we've focused on how to cite authority. However, the law isn't the only material that comes from external sources. The facts also come from external sources. And just as legal readers use the citations in your document to locate and verify the authority you've cited, legal readers also need citations to locate and verify the facts and allegations to which you apply the law in your analysis. Those facts are recorded in a variety of court documents, and those court documents compose what's called the "record" of the case. To fully understand what the record is, you need to first know how documents make their way into the record. Although specific practices vary from jurisdiction to jurisdiction, the general practice of accumulating the record is similar across the country. This chapter will use civil actions in federal courts for illustration.

The first document filed in a case is, of course, the complaint. When a document is "filed," that means it has been submitted to the clerk's office for that court. The clerk's office will start a file for that case and assign it a number. That number is called the "docket number." From that point forward, all documents filed in that case should have that number printed on them, and all documents will be placed in that file in chronological order behind the complaint. Therefore, the next document in the file behind the complaint will likely be some responsive pleading by the defendant. After the initial pleadings in the case, discovery documents (such as interrogatories) and a variety of motions and responses will be filed as they are submitted in the case.

## A. Citing Documents During the Trial Process

While the case makes its way through the trial process, the parties may want to refer back to documents already filed. For example, a Motion for Summary Judgment might refer back to allegations in the Complaint. When the allegations from the Complaint are referenced, the writer will need to cite the Complaint. *The Bluebook* quick reference for citing court documents is B10 of the Bluepages. Read B10 (including B10.1 through B10.6.3) before continuing with this chapter.

The first part of a court document citation is the abbreviated name of the document. For guidance in forming abbreviations for court documents, use BT.1 on page 25. BT1 contains abbreviations for words commonly found in court document titles. BT.1 also instructs you to omit articles and prepositions from any title. Although BT.1 does not guide you on whether to abbreviate ordinals (first, second, third, etc.), one of the primary goals of citation is to make the citation as short as possible while still conveying as much information as possible. In that spirit, then, abbreviate ordinals in document names just as you do for reporter and court abbreviations (1st, 2d, 3d, etc.).

| | |
|---|---|
| | Defendant's Brief in Support of Motion for Summary Judgment |
| becomes: | Def.'s Br. Supp. Mot. Summ. J. |
| | Plaintiff's Motion to Compel |
| becomes: | Pl.'s Mot. Compel |

Further, the name of the party filing the document is only necessary if both parties would be permitted to file the document under the applicable rules of procedure.

| | |
|---|---|
| | Def.'s Mot. Summ. J. |
| but NOT: | Def.'s Answer |

For affidavits and depositions, identify the documents by the affiant's or deponent's surname and the abbreviation for the document.

(St. James Dep. at 37.)

(Wells Aff. ¶ 12.)

The second part of the court document citation is the specific location of the material cited. B10.3 encourages as much specificity as possible.

| | |
|---|---|
| *cited by para. number* | (Doc. Name ¶ X.) |
| *cited by pg. number* | (Doc. Name X.) |
| *cited by line number* | (Doc Name pgX:lineX.) |
| *cited by item number* | (Doc. Name # X.) |

The third part of a court document citation is the date, when needed for clarity. If a party has given more than one deposition or affidavit, identify the document by date as well.

(Wells Aff. ¶ 12, July 14, 2005.)

Similarly, if many of the same type of documents have been filed (*e.g.*, Motion to Compel, Motion to Quash), specifying the date of the document may help to prevent reader confusion.

Finally, notice that citations to court documents, unlike citations to authority, are enclosed in parentheses. Even though the citation is enclosed in parentheses, it is still considered a citation sentence, and the period is placed just inside the closing parenthesis. However, if the record cite is in a citation clause, it will not contain a period.

Dr. Carter admits that his treatment plan was unorthodox (Answer ¶ 12) but denies that it was negligent (Carter Dep. at 73).

Rule B10.5 tells you that you should use a short form after the first full cite to a court document. Although B10.5 does not give specific rules for shortening court document cites, the examples suggest two common sense solutions: (1) omit dates from short forms, and (2) drop elements of the document name.

Essentially, any short form that sufficiently identifies a lengthy document name would be acceptable.

| | |
|---|---|
| *full form:* | (Def.'s Br. Supp. Mot. Summ. J. at 39.) |
| *short form:* | (Def.'s Br. Supp. at 45.) |

Additionally, rule 4.1 does say that " '*Id.* ' may be used in citation sentences and clauses for any kind of authority." Just as with other cites to factual, rather than legal, authority, the citation should be inside parentheses.

(*Id.*)

## B. Citing Documents on Appeal

When an appellate court considers a case, it may have access to three different types of factual information: the record, the transcript of testimony, and exhibits offered at trial.

When a case begins the appellate process, documents filed with the trial court clerk's office are referred to as part of the record ("R.") rather than as individual documents (*e.g.*, "Pl.'s Mot. Compel"). The documents in the clerk's file are consecutively numbered, beginning with the complaint and ending with the last document in the case. At that point, all material is referenced by page number rather than paragraph number. Therefore, the Complaint might have been cited like this during the course of the trial:

(Compl. ¶ 3.)

However, when the parties refer to the Complaint in the appellate briefs, it would be cited like this:

(R. at 1.)

The transcript of trial testimony may be cited as "Tr." and specific material within a transcript may be referred to by page number.

(Tr. at 39.)

The exhibits admitted during trial are cited as "Ex." and bear the abbreviation of the party that offered the exhibit and the number of the exhibit.

(Def.'s Ex. 12.)

## C. Texas Record on Appeal[1]

*Texas Rules of Form* does not follow B10 of *The Bluebook* with regard to citation of the record on appeal. Therefore, lawyers before Texas state courts must know how to cite using both *Bluebook* rule B10 and *Texas Rules of Form* rule 7.2. Read rule 7.2 before continuing with this chapter.

Rule 7.2 indicates that both the documents collected by the court clerk and the transcription of trial testimony are called the "record." However, one is the "clerk's record," and the other is the "court reporter's record." Documents found in the court clerk's file for the case should be cited as the clerk's record.

(C.R. at 12).

Documents found in the transcript of trial testimony should be cited as the court reporter's record.

(R.R. at 189).

If the clerk's record or the reporter's record is too large for a single volume, the records may be divided into multiple volumes and labeled consecutively with roman numerals. Those volume numbers are placed in the citation before the record abbreviation.

(II C.R. at 46).

(IV R.R. at 39).

Notice that *Texas Rules of Form* requires that citations to the record be in parentheses, just as *The Bluebook* does. However, unlike *The Bluebook*, *Texas Rules of Form* instructs you to include the record cite as part of the textual sentence rather than creating a separate citation sentence.

---

[1] This section addresses records created on or after September 1, 1997. To cite a record created before September 1, 1997, consult rule 7.2.2 of *Texas Rules of Form*.

| | |
|---|---|
| *Bluebook*: | Defendant's car failed to yield the right of way. (Tr. at 57.) |
| *TROF*: | Defendant's car failed to yield the right of way (R.R. at 57). |

With regard to exhibits, *Texas Rules of Form* is very similar to *Bluebook* B10. However, it does add that, when there are more than two parties involved in an action, the exhibits should be identified by the party's name rather than abbreviated procedural label.

And there you have it! For the record, you're ready for the exercise.

# Exercise 18
# Court Documents

## A. Court Documents: Trial & Appellate

Put the following information in correct *Bluebook* citation form. All sources are being cited in citation sentences in a brief to a federal district court. This exercise focuses on B10. You will also need to refer to BT.1 for abbreviations of words commonly used in court document titles.

**1.** In a Motion to Compel Production of Documents, you wish to cite page 2 of Plaintiff's Request for Production. To date in this litigation, the Plaintiff has only filed one Request for Production.

**2.** Without any intervening cites, you again want to cite to page 2, of Plaintiff's Request for Production.

**3.** In the same Motion to Compel mentioned in #1 above, you wish to cite to paragraph 7 of Plaintiff's Original Complaint.

**4.** In an appellate brief, you wish to cite to the fourth paragraph of Defendant's First Amended Answer.

**5.** In a Motion for Summary Judgment, you wish to cite to paragraph 2 of the one-page affidavit of Mark Wellbury, M.S.N., M.P.H. This is the only affidavit given by Mr. Wellbury.

**6.** In a Motion for New Trial, you wish to cite to Plaintiff's Exhibit 4.

7. Two paragraphs later, in the same Motion for New Trial, you wish to cite to the deposition testimony of Rhoda McGaven.

______________________________________________

______________________________________________

______________________________________________

8. On page 8 of the same Motion for New Trial, you wish to cite to the Court's Verdict. In the consecutively-numbered record kept by the court clerk, the verdict is on page 472.

______________________________________________

______________________________________________

______________________________________________

## B. Texas Record on Appeal

Put the following information in correct *Texas Rules of Form* citation form. All sources are being cited in citation sentences in an appellate brief to a state court of appeals. This exercise focuses on Rule 7.2.

**1.** You wish to cite to State's Exhibit 18.

**2.** You wish to cite page 7 of the Plaintiff's Motion to Compel Production of Documents, *which appears on page 43 of the Court Clerk's record.* [Note: the italicized material was inadvertently left out of the workbook text for the problem]

**3.** You wish to cite the trial testimony of Raymond T. Wilcox, found on page 23 of the single-volume reporter's record.

**4.** In the same document as #3 above, you wish to cite exhibit 23, introduced by the third-party defendant, Texaco, Inc.

**5.** In response to Defendant's Special Exceptions, you wish to cite paragraph 6 of that document, *which appears on page 15 of the Court Clerk's record.* [Note: the italicized material was inadvertently left out of the workbook text for the problem]

**6.** You wish to cite the trial testimony of Judith Holmes, M.D., whose testimony appears on page 33 of volume IV of the transcription of trial testimony.

**7.** In the immediately following sentence, you wish to cite to Holmes's testimony appearing on page 35 of volume IV of the transcription of trial testimony.

______________________________________________

______________________________________________

______________________________________________